BEEKEEPING

Originally published in Sweden by Bonnier Fakta in 2015
as *Bisyssla om bin, biodling och biprodukter*
Text © Joachim Petterson, 2015
Photographs © Roland Persson
(excepting pages 59, 93, 161,162–16 Emma Shevtzoff,
85 Joachim Petterson, and 70 and 119 Sara Petterson)
Illustrations © SaraMara, www.sara-mara.se
(excepting page 117 Svea and Göta Petterson)
Graphic Design Joachim Petterson, www.honeydesign.se
Editor Susanna Eriksson Lundqvist
Repro JK Morris Production AB, Värnamo

weldon**owen**
P.O. Box 3088
San Rafael, CA 94912
www.weldonowen.com

President & Publisher Roger Shaw
Associate Publisher Mariah Bear
Associate Editor Ian Cannon
Editorial Assistant Molly O'Neil Stewart
Creative Director Kelly Booth
Senior Production Designer Rachel Lopez Metzger
Production Director Chris Hemesath
Associate Production Director Michelle Duggan

Weldon Owen would like to thank Jeri Martinez for fact-checking,
Brittany Bogan for proofreading, and Kevin Broccoli of BIM Creatives for the index.

Library of Congress Cataloging in Publication data is available.

This edition first printed in 2016
10 9 8 7 6

ISBN 13: 978-1-68188-154-6
ISBN 10: 1-68188-154-3

Printed in China

BEEKEEPING

A HANDBOOK ON HONEY, HIVES & HELPING THE BEES

Joachim Petterson

Photography by Roland Persson

Illustrations by SaraMara
Translated by Victoria Haggblom

weldonowen

A large group of worker bees gathered at the hive entrance. They work together to reduce heat in the hive by fanning their wings.

CONTENTS

MY BEES

When I became a beekeeper, there wasn't as much interest
in beekeeping as there is now. Today, there's an increased
understanding for the importance of bees' health; the threat
to their existence is a global concern. The pollination that
bees and bumblebees perform is crucial to human survival.
Two-thirds of everything we eat is dependent on this important
activity, which doesn't cost us a cent.

My interest in beekeeping was kindled when, as a child,
I visited my great-uncle in Värmland, Sweden. He told me bees
lived in the little white houses placed a little way from the farm,
and he showed me how to harvest honey. It seemed exciting,
harmonious, and cozily domestic to be a beekeeper. I can still
recall the sweet scent of wax and honey when I snuck into the
room where the honey extractor stood. It would take almost
thirty years before I became a beekeeper, with hives of my own.

I went to school for advertising and graphic design. After
graduating, I worked as an art director for large and small
advertising agencies. My career took off; I had eminent clients
and received several awards in excellence for my work. My life
spun faster and faster and at one point, one of the senior directors
at my firm grabbed my arm and told me to go home and get
some sleep: "No one's going to thank you for getting a heart
attack." Those words would come to mean a lot to me later on.

In the fall of 2002, my life came to a complete halt. I suffered
a head trauma after a fall of ten meters and needed years of
rehabilitation; this gave me time to reflect. I began reevaluating
what is truly important and meaningful in life. Within a year,
I also became a father and bought a house. One of the things
I decided to do then was to finish a project I'd spent many
woodworking hours on in junior high, but never completed:
I was going to finish the beehive that stood in the garage and
find out whether beekeeping was something for me. I took
a class on beekeeping, bought every book available on the
subject, and asked my experienced beekeeping relatives for

advice. Then, I placed my new hive in an appropriately sunny spot in my garden and introduced the bee colony I'd bought from a beekeeper nearby. I'd reached my first goal.

Today, I live with my family, my wife Sara and our daughters Svea and Göta in Stockholm, Sweden. I have five active hives in my garden; this number is manageable in terms of work, and yields enough honey to cover our family's needs and more. As a beekeeper, you are amply rewarded for the time you spend on your bees. For me, it's not just about the honey. To work with the bees, feel their warmth, and inhale the scent of wax and honey is contemplative and has a therapeutic effect. It's calming to just sit by the hives, to see the bees communicate with their dances, and study how the colony develops with the season. Beekeeping also makes me feel closer to nature and it is satisfying to know that I'm doing something good that brings others joy as well. When I see the trees in my neighborhood overflowing with fruit, I know that it's partly because of my bees that the fruits are so big and plentiful.

My intention was to write an inspiring and practical book for everyone interested in bees and who might want to start getting involved right away. You don't have to become a beekeeper to help our pollinating friends, either. For example, you can attract more bees and bumblebees to your garden by building nests and establishing plants they like.

To tell others that you are a beekeeper is a great icebreaker at dinners and parties. I often get questions about bees and their health, but many conversations are also about honey. We need lots more beekeepers to help ensure we have plenty of healthy bees. I'd rather see that we get a hundred new beekeepers with a couple of hives each in various places than just one beekeeper with a hundred hives in one location.

It might seem odd but, as a beekeeper, you really get attached to your fuzzy friends. When I'm sitting by the hive in the spring sunshine, watching one bee after another land with their load of pollen on the entrance cleat and wander into the hive, it almost seems to me that they are unique individuals and not just part of a larger collective organism.

CHAPTER ONE

PROTECTING THE BEES

Bees, bumblebees, and other insects have one of
the most important tasks in the world: pollination—the
fertilization of our plants. Their tireless work increases
our harvests and also benefits the plants that sustain
many animal species. This is a service human beings
take advantage of every day, and it's free.

POLLINATION FOR BILLIONS

A majority of pollinating insects are honeybees, which live in large colonies. In one day, honeybees from one single hive gather energy-rich and protein-filled pollen from over 100,000 flowers and simultaneously spread pollen from one flower to another. When the bees rummage around inside the flowers and suck up their nectar, some of the pollen is transferred from the anthers to the stigma and fertilize it. The rest of the pollen sticks to the bees' legs and is brought home to the hive alone with the nectar, which then becomes honey. Half a million flower visits are needed to make one teaspoon of honey. Pollination can also occur with the help of wind, insects, other animals, and sometimes humans. There is no question regarding which of these methods is the most cost-effective.

The ecological balance in nature is intricate, but if conditions change, plants and animals can often adjust to their new circumstances. Historically, bees have been strong survivors, but today, the world is changing so rapidly and dramatically that many bee species are threatened by extinction. Fewer bee species lead to less seeds in many crops and thereby decreased harvests. It is a matter of high importance that we pause and take heed. We have to change—the bees won't change their behavior.

It was in October 2006 that the first alarming news about a rapid, widespread disappearance of vast numbers of bee colonies was reported in the United States. This phenomenon would later become known as Colony Collapse Disorder, or CCD. The notion of massive bee deaths was soon spread in the media, inaccurately, since the growth of honeybees is still stable worldwide—even in the United States. On the other hand, huge colony losses have occurred in many places for various reasons.

There are several different theories and probably many various reasons for the many losses of bee colonies. The heavy use of pesticides in farming and the preventative treatment of bees with antibiotics have been discussed as potential causes. Another important factor could be that the bees' pollination work is of huge financial importance. In the United States, bee colonies are transported in eighteen-wheelers back and forth across the continent between flowering seasons to perform pollination work worth billions of dollars. I'm convinced that bees can become stressed and more susceptible to disease if they are forced to live in an environment they are not adapted to.

Varroa mites have been identified as a major reason for why bee colonies die during the winter. But another reason could be neglect in caring for the colony, which could lead to the bees freezing or starving to death because they weren't given enough food for winter. In general, the monoculture that has reduced plant diversity globally has also impacted honeybees and other pollinators negatively. The use of chemicals has increased and many plants are being treated with insecticides while still in their seed state. The toxins are stored in plants and transferred to the pollen and nectar, which the bees bring back to the hive to feed their larvae. Another potential threat can be that the bees risk new enemies and diseases as a result of the intercontinental transport of produce and other products from different parts of the world.

In some places in the world, humans have had to take over the role of the bees. In China's most famous fruit-growing area, the Sichuan province, the aggressive use of chemical pesticides has resulted in the farmers moving their bees away from the heavily sprayed crops. In order to get good crops, they have to perform the pollination by hand, with small brushes.

It's easy to get depressed by alarming reports and dismal predictions for the future. The solutions might seem distant and complicated, but even small acts of support can make a big difference for honeybees and other pollinating insects. One way to improve their conditions is to invite them into our gardens. Today, close to one in ten bee species are threatened with extinction and 5.2 percent risk of becoming endangered in the near future.

HONEYBEES, BUMBLEBEES, AND SOLITARY BEES

Eighty percent of all living things on Earth are insects. Humans have found ways to use some of them, such as breeding silk worms to produce raw silk—a tradition 5,000 years old—or keeping bees to produce wax and honey. There are about 17,000 species of bee; only a few live in colonies and produce honey. Among them are honeybees (*Apis*), bumblebees (*Bombus*), and stingless bees (*Meliponini*). These are all social bees belonging to the order *Hymenoptera*. The remaining species are solitary bees, for example: mason bees, miner bees, carpenter bees, and leaf-cutting bees.

Honeybees

Most people associate bees with honeybees, which live in hives and gather nectar to make honey. Their colonies include an egg-producing queen, drones (males), and workers (infertile females). Colony structure is described in detail in the next chapter.

For a long time, only four bee species, including their subspecies, had been identified: the Western bee, the Eastern bee, Dwarf bees, and Giant bees. Today, nine species of colony bees have been identified; five of these are bees of normal size who build parallel waxcombs inside hollow spaces (*Apis mellifera, A. cerana, A. nigrocincta, A. koschevnikovi,* and *A. nuluensis*); two are dwarf bees (*A. florea* and *A. andreniformis*); and two are Giant bees (*A. dorsata* and *A. d. laboriosa*), who prefer to build their colonies in big, freely hanging honeycombs rather than inside hollows.

In different parts of the world, different bee species have developed traits and temperaments especially adapted to area in which they live. The Western bee, *A. mellifera,* originated in Africa and Europe, spreading in great numbers toward the Ural Mountains. Thanks to humans, it is now found worldwide, even in the Americas and Australia, where *Apis* previously wasn't found at all. Today, *A. mellifera* is the most common honeybee in the world, probably because it's the easiest one to keep. In Europe,

there are no other species of honeybees than *A. mellifera,* and over tens of thousands of years, several subspecies have developed.

Apis mellifera mellifera, the black honeybee, or the dark honeybee, has lived on the European continent since the Ice Age. It has the largest geographical span of all bees and has become a generalized species in Europe with local names such as English honeybee, German honeybee, Nordic honeybee, and so on. On the Iberian Peninsula lives the native species *A. m. iberica,* closely related to the black honeybee. *Apis m. ligustica,* the yellow Italian bee, has its origins in the Apennine peninsula, where it developed in a rather isolated environment. A stone's throw from there, we'll find *A. m. carnica,* the Carnica honeybee, which used to be called the Krainer honeybee after the town Krain in Slovenia. This is the most common honeybee in the east, toward the Carpathian Mountains, Bulgaria, and the Ukraine. To the South, we find the Macedonian honeybee: *A. m. Macedonia,* as well as the Greek: *A. m. cecropia*. In Sweden, there are mainly three species in hives: dark European honeybees, yellow Ligustica honeybee (Italian), and grayish Carnolian honeybees. In addition, another bred sub-species is often found: the brownish buckfast honeybee. Different breeds have varying characteristics and each breed has its own enthusiasts.

In some places, honeybees are almost seen as pets. But we'll never be able to "domesticate" them; we've only learned how to make them feel comfortable around us.

Bumblebees

Like honeybees, bumblebees are important pollinators in both the wild and in cultivated gardens. They, too, live in colonies with a queen, but on a much smaller scale, and they like to build their nests in holes in the ground or among rocks. Their furry bodies make them less sensitive to weather changes, so they're active early in the spring season when it's still a bit chilly outside. Bumblebees don't fly far, so they're good to have around if you want extra help with pollination in your garden early in spring.

A British study has shown that bumblebee colonies in cities grow faster than those placed in conventional agricultural

A scientific mistake

Carl Linnaeus named the honeybee *Apis mellifera* (after the Latin word *apis* = bee, *mel* = honey and *ferre* = to carry) because he thought bees carried honey to the hive. Later, when he realized that bees actually make honey from the nectar, he wanted to change the name to *Apis mellifica,* which means "maker of honey" (*facere* = to do), but this was not approved; according to scientific naming rules, the first name given to a species should always be used.

Bumblebees in the greenhouse

Bumblebees have long been bred to perform pollination in greenhouses. This practice has become so successful that in many countries, you can now get bumblebee colonies in cardboard boxes via mail order for your greenhouse.

landscapes. This strongly suggests that it's beneficial to create more homes for them in our urban gardens.

Solitary bees

Some bee species are solitary bees that don't live in colonies or hives and don't produce honey; they use nectar only as fuel for flying. On the other hand, they do us a great service when they fly around from flower to flower and gather pollen.

Some species are specialists, choosing only one flower type when seeking nourishment, but most select a variety of plants. Since they have no colony to defend, solitary bees have developed a soft stinger, which they rarely use. Unlike bees in colonies, all females are fertile and can lay eggs. A fertilized female looks for a suitable hollow where she lays her egg that develops into a larvae, then a pupa, and finally a bee. Some species can hibernate as pupae and hatch in summer; others hibernate in their holes as adult bees, waiting in their nests until the air warms, preferably to above 60 °F (15 °C), when it's time for their first flight. Most solitary bee species lay their eggs in hollows in the ground; some choose to lay them in cracks of dead wood. They use spaces other insects have already created or those naturally occurring in plants with porous structures, such as elderberry or raspberry bushes. Unfortunately, solitary bees have an increasingly difficult time finding natural habitats, which has led to several species disappearing or become drastically reduced.

DON'T BLAME THE BEES

People often think that it's bees buzzing around their outside dining table in the summer, trying to get into their juice glass, or the sugar for their coffee, on their cake, or on the newly grilled steak, but the real culprits are wasps, who look deceptively like bees at first glance. They can be a nuisance, but wasps pollinate our plants similar to bees. Wasps are also carnivores and reduce the number of harmful insects in our gardens. Before you start yelling at a beekeeping neighbor, here's how to tell the two apart.

There is a difference between bees and wasps

BEES

. . . have dark brown, grayish or yellow-brown, fuzzy bodies and hairy legs.

. . . are vegetarian and only interested in gathering flower pollen and nectar to make honey. That's why they're rarely seen around our outside dining tables.

. . . live in hives or build nests in hollows with vertical honeycombs. If they were to build a nest inside a wall it wouldn't cause any structural damage.

. . . hibernate in the colony with their queen. When spring comes, the queen starts to lay eggs while the worker bees feed the larvae, clean, build honeycombs, guard the hive, and gather food.

. . . are not aggressive, but if they feel threatened, they may attack. They only use their stinger in an emergency; it has tiny barbs that can easily get caught in skin and then tear out the venom sac. This will kill the bee.

WASPS

. . . have clear yellow and black patterning and their narrow bodies look shiny.

. . . are omnivores that eat meat, fish, fruit, and sweet drinks, i.e. all those things we like to eat for outside lunches or barbecues in the summer.

. . . often build round nests of chewed-up wood. They scrape off wood fibers with their jaws and then chew and mix it with saliva, turning it into cellulose.

. . . only live for one summer. Only the wasp queen hibernates during the winter. In the spring, she finds a new place to live and builds her own nest, lays eggs, and feeds the larvae.

. . . generally only sting if they have been attacked or scared. Unlike bees, their stinger is not barbed, so they can sting repeatedly—and they also bite. If the wasps don't bother or harm you, simply leave them alone!

BEE PLANTS AND DRAW PLANTS

Bees collect nectar and pollen from flowering trees, shrubs, and herbs. The amount and distribution varies between different plant species. The phrase bee plants refers to all flowering plants that are particularly important to pollinating insects. In general, it means all kinds of plants that have something that bees can bring back to the hive: high-protein pollen or sweet nectar. Fruit trees, berry bushes, many perennials, and most edible herbs are bee plants, as well as some tree species such as maple, crab apple and chestnut. One strange phenomenon is that trees that bloom in the late summer may be surrounded by dazed or dead bees and bumblebees on the ground. Why this happens is unclear, but it has been speculated that the bees are so weak late in the season that they die from exhaustion caused by their intense collecting in preparation for the winter. This can happen particularly in areas with European linden trees or California buckeye trees.

Even plants that don't have a lot of pollen or nectar can be vital food sources for bees if they bloom in early spring or during other periods when there isn't a lot of food around. Plants that yield so much nectar and pollen that they can dominate bees' nutritional intake for periods of time are called draw plants. In early spring, sallow is the most important draw plant. Typical draw plants in early summer are dandelion, rapeseed, turnip rape, raspberry and clover. In late summer, it can be phacelia, linden, fireweed, and heather. Trees such as linden, maple, and some conifers are particularly important to bees because they are often attacked by aphids that excrete honeydew after eating plants. In addition to honeydew, many other deciduous and coniferous plants such as spruce and fir contribute with resin, which bees use to make propolis. If you plant edible herbs in your garden or windowbox, both you and the bees have much to enjoy. Depending on the local climate, almost all edible herbs bloom in July, with many small flowers that give a lot of nectar.

From sallow to heather

Solitary bees and bumblebees mainly search for plants that provide quick and easily accessible food. Honeybees are more structured and focus on one food source at a time. The plants that provide the first pollen of the year are often alder and hazel. In their catkins are large amounts of pollen with quite a high protein content. Soon after, sallows will bloom and their yellow catkins are like magnets to newly awakened bumblebees and other bees in great need of replenishing their food stores after the long winter. Sallow contains lots of protein-rich pollen and energy-filled nectar, making it a key plant for beekeeping, and can bloom as early as February. Many gardeners consider sallow to be a pest and don't hesitate cutting it down. But think of its importance to the bees when you are out clearing brushwood. When the sallow blossoms is when the bees really begin to work in earnest, so if you have room in your garden, consider leaving some sallow bushes rather than removing them.

Among the early spring flowers, the wood anemone is an important draw plant that contains lots of pollen (but not a lot of nectar). In just one day, a brownish forest slope can transform into a sea of white flowers full of pollen. Wood anemones bloom in April and May. Dandelion is also an early draw plant that is appreciated by bees and beekeepers, but which people detest and call a weed. Dandelions flower starting in early May and spread

Dandelion

Sallow Wood Anemone

rapidly. They produce large amounts of valuable pollen and nectar that can provide bees with the year's first surplus of honey. If the bees collect most of the nectar they need from dandelions, the honey can turn out bright yellow—dandelion honey.

Another yellow plant that comes early in the season is rapeseed. Unlike dandelion honey, rapeseed honey is almost white. When the rapeseed blossoms, the draw period begins in earnest and the bees can collect large stores of honey.

In mid-May, it's time for the important flowering trees: cherry and apple with their masses of pink and white flowers, closely followed by all sorts of berry bushes that demand the bees' attention. In late May and early June, one pollen and nectar rich source after another blossom in nature and in gardens— hawthorn, forget-me-not, cornflowers, and many more.

During June and July is when the most nectar and pollen is collected. Some bee plants stand out more than others. Different kinds of clover blossoms are important sources of nectar; they also capture nitrogen in the air to fertilize the soil in which they grow. Raspberry is another good bee plant that blossoms throughout most of the summer, both in gardens and wild in clearcuts. In late summer, bees seek out late flowering edible herbs, fireweed, phacelia, and orpine. One of the very last draw plants of the season is heather.

Apple blossom

Cornflower

Dandelion

A bee friendly garden

If you start an apiary, you're helping the environment, but there are additional things you can do to increase the survival rate of pollinating insects. One way is to transform your garden into a nutritious oasis by growing pollen- and nectar-rich plants. You're then doing something to compensate for the fact that it has become increasingly difficult for bees, bumblebees, and other insects to find food due to large-scale agriculture with crops that rarely or never blossom. If you plant bee-friendly plants in your garden, you're not only helping the insects; it will also give you an opulent garden. The insects pollinate the plants and make sure you get more flowers, berries, and fruits. For example, each time a bee visits an apple blossom, it will create a new seed and with each new seed, the fruit will get bigger. Another positive effect is that green plants produce oxygen, which cleans the air, removing the greenhouse gas carbon monoxide. The more bee-friendly flowering plants you have in your garden, the better. We have planted phacelia and white clover in our lawn. We've also created a late-summer flowerbed and planted a butterfly bush, which is visited by bees, flower flies, and butterflies into September.

Inquire at the nursery about which plants the bees prefer and what works best for your climate zone, as well as for the specific conditions in your garden. If you want to grow plants in pots, you can choose exotic flowers, which the bees love. Find the sunniest spot in your garden—that's where bees, bumblebees, and butterflies like to be. Then plant the flowers in various groups. Choose plants with flowers in varying colors and sizes; this will attract more species. Blue, purple, yellow, and white flowers are most popular. Also, make sure your plants blossom at different times during the flowering season, and combine them with those that flower for a longer time. This will create biodiversity in a micro-format and the bees will have access to a rich and varied selection of nectar and pollen from early spring until fall.

A traditional green lawn may impress some neighbors, but
I think of it as boring and uninspiring, especially since there's
almost nothing for pollinating insects. A well-groomed lawn has
few plants that provide pollen and nectar. I avoid mowing the
lawn before midsummer and often tell others to do the same.
If you have to cut the grass, try to at least leave some of the lawn
unkempt. Every year, we let a sunny part of our garden grow
wild and turn into a lovely summer meadow. Both wildflowers
and the meadow plants we've added to the lawn spread easily and
benefit our bees as well as butterflies and bumblebees. You can
find seeds for local wildflowers in almost all nurseries.

   If you don't mow your lawn very much during summer, it's
especially good to plant white clover. White clover is a great plant
for bees since it has an extended period of bloom and contains
lots of nectar and pollen. Because it is nitrogen-fixing, it is also
less susceptible to drought than grass.

   Planting bulbs in the lawn in autumn also benefits the bees.
Bulbs are important because they bloom in early spring when
there are few sources for pollen and nectar. Plant species that
can spread easily, such as winter aconite, snowdrop, scilla, spring
star, and crocus. Then simply leave the flowers alone when they
bloom, and do not cut the grass until they have wilted down.

If you don't have a garden but own a balcony, you can help the bees by growing draw plants in pots or plant boxes. This will create a pleasant oasis that will reduce stress both in you and the city bees. It's actually possible to establish an apiary on a rooftop or large balcony. If you don't have a balcony, you can at least hang a flower box outside one of your windows. Agricultural pesticides affect bees negatively, so always buy organic plants, use only untreated soil without toxins, and don't use chemical pesticides. If you're using fertilizer, make sure you know what it contains. Make your own compost from household waste and use it in your flowerbeds. There is an easy and odorless Japanese composting method, called Bokashi, that you can use under the kitchen sink of your apartment.

Aside from pollen and nectar, pollinating insects need water, so placing a birdbath in the garden is a great idea. Add some stones or glass marbles to a large bowl of water and let them stick up above the surface so that the bees can access the water without drowning. You can also put some floating leca clay pellets in the water. If you have the space, you can also establish a nice pond, where bees and other residents in the garden can all go to quench their thirst.

Plant a Buffet for Bees

No matter where in the U.S. you live, you can plant a bee-friendly garden to help nourish your hive or other local bees. Bees appreciate a varied diet as much as we do, so mix it up and plant a nice selection for them to choose from. The plants pictured below are a sampling of the hundreds of options available to you. The best plant for local conditions will vary widely throughout the Americas, but this is a good start. Check with your friendly neighborhood garden center or beekeepers association to learn which flowers will grow best in your region.

Annuals

Cosmos (HHA)
Many species

Borage
Borago officinalis

Sunflowers
Helianthus annuus

Snapdragons
Many species

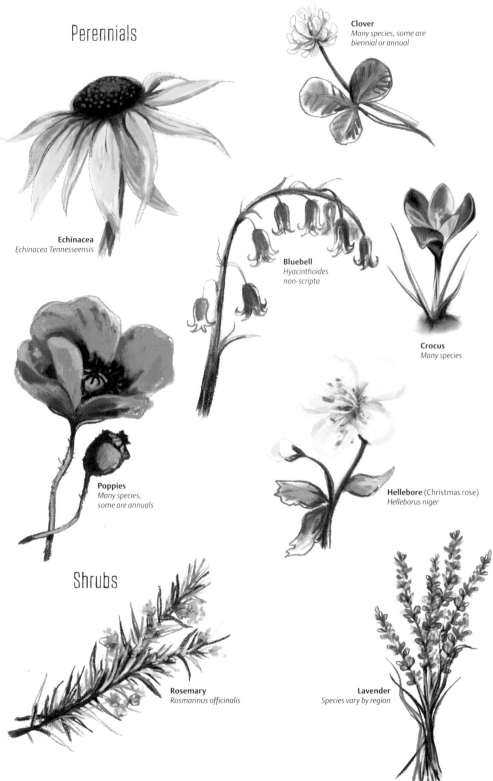

Perennials

Clover
Many species, some are biennial or annual

Echinacea
Echinacea Tennesseensis

Bluebell
Hyacinthoides non-scripta

Crocus
Many species

Poppies
Many species, some are annuals

Hellebore (Christmas rose)
Helleborus niger

Shrubs

Rosemary
Rosmarinus officinalis

Lavender
Species vary by region

HABITATS FOR WILD BEES

In addition to attracting wild bees and bumblebees to your garden by planting lots of different flowers, you can also help them establish nests and thereby increase their chances of survival. Solitary bees and bumblebees are avid pollinators, but they don't fly as far as honeybees. This means that if they establish a nest in your garden, they can become a real asset since they will pollinate all your trees, bushes, and flowers. If you have elderberry or raspberry in your garden or there are reeds nearby, you can easily make simple "bee batteries" where the insects can establish a nest. From scrap wood, you can build bee houses that look like high-rises for bees. You can also make nests for bumblebees, or why not an entire insect hotel with a spa?

Bee batteries

You can make a bee battery from hollow elderberry- or raspberry canes or from a bundle of reeds. If you want to use a firmer material, bamboo is a good choice. You can find it in varying sizes in garden supply stores and nurseries. Cut the canes, reeds, or bamboo into 8- to 12-inch (20–30-cm) pieces. Then tie 10 to 20 of them into a bundle with a piece of string. If you use bamboo, make sure that the node (the section on the bamboo where it is closed up inside) ends up somewhere in the middle so the hole doesn't go all the way through the bamboo shaft.

You can place the bee batteries in different spots in the garden. The bees prefer that you hang them on a wall facing south; you can also place them on a big rock or among a pile of rocks, where you can study your new guests. You can also tie the batteries to a tree trunk or a small branch. It's important to make sure that the bee batteries are not exposed to moisture directly from the ground.

You can make a simple and stylish larger bee nest by perforating the end of a log or a piece of firewood with a drill. Make several holes of varying sizes from 0.1 to 0.5 inches (0.25–1.25 cm). The wood has to be dry, otherwise the holes can get frayed and the bees don't like that.

Now you can study which size holes that different species prefer. A diameter of 0.43 inches (1.1 cm) is ideal for bees that visit apple blossoms, so if you have many apple trees that need pollinating, try using this size. You can experiment and see which flowers in your garden your different tenants prefer.

When you're finished with your battery, place it on a wall or on a firm surface, but never directly on the ground. It's good to find a spot with mostly sun but some hours of shade during the day, otherwise it'll get too hot. Solitary bees like both morning and evening sun.

If you want to paint your bee batteries, remember that bees can orient themselves easier if you use simple geometrical figures, for example crosses and circles, and bright, contrasting colors. They discern blue and purple shades clearly while red is perceived as black. Make sure to use non-toxic paint!

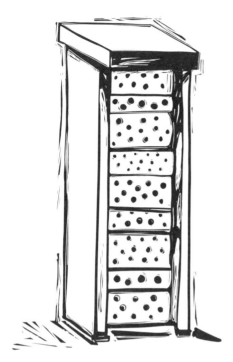

Bee houses or bee hotels

If you happen to have untreated, flat scrap wood around, you can easily build both large and small bee houses; or why not a bee hotel with room for 100 solitary bees?

Cut ten pieces of flat wood into equally large sizes, preferably 4 inches (10 cm) long. Drill holes that are 0.1 to 0.5 inches (0.25–1.25 cm) in diameter in the short ends of each piece. Two pieces should have ten holes that are 0.1 inches (0.25 cm) wide, two with ten holes that are 0.2 inches (0.5 cm) wide, etc.

Place the pieces on top of each other so you have a high pile and then nail on sidepieces and an angled roof, so water can run off the top.

Insect hotel with spa

To assist several species of pollinating insects, you can combine various types of habitats for solitary bees, bumblebees, and other insects under one roof.

Using untreated wood, make a large box with a back cover, floors, walls, ceilings and partitions. The box should have a minimum depth of 4 inches (10 cm). Place different nesting materials—for example, pine cones, bark, sawdust, bamboo sticks, or small wood pieces with drilled holes—in the "rooms." Cover the front with chicken wire to protect against birds. As a fun feature, you can set a small dish of water on the ground floor; now, the bees have their own spa. If you are short on time or if carpentry isn't your strong suit, there are bee nests and insect hotels in many designs and various sizes available for purchase in different price ranges in garden stores and from online retailers.

Bumblebee nests

In early spring when the sun begins to warm the ground, the bumblebee queen sets out to find a suitable burrow to lay her eggs in. If you don't have old vole tunnels in your garden—which provide plenty of nest space for bumblebees—you can make a nest for the queen by burying a clay pot upside down in the ground. The pot should be at least 6 inches (15 cm) in diameter and have a hole in the bottom. Choose a location that is sunny, preferably with some protective vegetation around it, and dig a hole as deep as the pot is high so that the bottom of the hole is positioned just above ground level. Fill the pot halfway with, for example, loosely packed straw, or sawdust from a pet store, before inserting it into the soil. Put a few small rocks over the opening to protect the entrance (the hole in the pot), but leave a small gap open for access.

CHAPTER TWO

LIFE IN THE COLONY

DRONE   QUEEN   WORKER BEE

Honey bees are social insects and live together in large communities, much like humans. A hive consists of about 50,000 individuals in one big family. Bees have to cooperate; without their colony, they can't survive. There are three kinds of bees in a colony, but they are completely interdependent on each other and function as one large super organism.

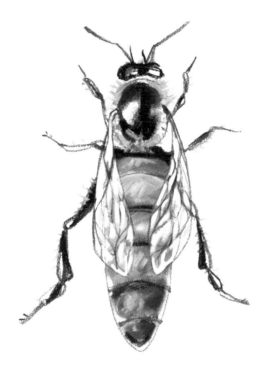

THE QUEEN—THE GREAT MATRIARCH

Bees live in a matriarchy; to put it simply, it's the queen that controls the colony. Her main task is procreation, but by exuding different scent signals (pheromones), she also controls many other activities in the hive. For example, she can affect construction activity by stimulating wax production in the building bees, which also increases the nurturing instinct of the bees that feed the larvae. There is normally only one queen in a colony, and she produces enormous amounts of eggs (or establishes cells, as it's also called) in her lifetime, nearly half a million. During peak season, she lays up to 3,000 eggs per day. Her daily egg production is equivalent to several times her own weight, and this requires large amounts of nutritious food. If you spot the queen the hive, you'll notice that she's constantly being attended to by worker bees feeding and preening her. The queen moves around across the honeycombs and "controls" what needs to be done in the colony with her scent signals.

A queen can live for four to five years, but she is most effective during her first and second years. Beekeepers therefore usually replace the queen after two to three years. If she perishes or if the colony isn't satisfied with her work, the worker bees instantly bring forth a successor. They select a young larva and build a cell for it that's several times larger than a normal cell (0.7 to 0.9 inches (1.8–2.3 cm)) and looks like a cocoon. There is no difference between the egg of a worker bee and the egg in a queen cell. However, the queen larvae are fed with a special nutritional juice called royal jelly. Sixteen days after the egg has been laid, a grown queen crawls out of the cell. About a week later, she flies out of the hive and mates in the air with up to about twenty drones. Back in the hive, her reproductive tract contains millions of sperm. The fertilized eggs are born as workers or queens, depending on what they are fed with; the unfertilized ones are born as drones.

Royal jelly

Working bees produce a protein-rich secretion, a feeding juice, which they use to raise the queen larvae. Because of the royal jelly, she develops into a bee almost twice as large as the other bees, has fully developed sexual organs, and lives up to three times longer. The royal jelly is extracted by beekeepers and sold in health food stores.

"THERE CAN BE ONLY ONE"

A QUEEN BEE USUALLY LIVES FOR 2–3 YEARS

IT TAKES 16 DAYS FOR AN EGG TO GROW INTO A MATURE QUEEN

The queen cell, also known as a supersedure cell, is greater than the normal cells of a honeycomb. It is built mostly on the outside of the honeycomb and is oriented downward.

DRONES—LAZY SUITORS

In a hive, there are a few hundred to a few thousand drones. They're the only male individuals in the hive and their main function is to mate with the queen. They don't participate in the daily work in the hive. But not all drones get to mate with the queen and the joy of the selected suitors is short-lived. After mating, the drones' genitals are torn out and they fall dead to the ground. The drones don't have stingers and they eat copious amounts of food. Those who don't mate with the queen live for an average of 45 days; 90 days at the most. Drones reach sexual maturity at 8 to 10 days of age. Drones are born in early summer and have a decent life until autumn approaches and the rest of the colony begins to tire of their lazy existence. The worker bees stop feeding the drones or simply throw them out of the hive. The drone has the longest development of all bee types in the hive. On the twenty-fourth day, it begins to chew its way out of its cell. About a week later, it's sexually mature and ready to mate.

A drone has a mother and a grandfather, but no father.

WORKER BEES—BUSY LADIES

Like the queen, worker bees are also female, but they are infertile since their ovaries aren't fully developed like the queen's. The worker bees are capable of producing eggs if there's no queen in the hive, but their offspring can only become drones, as their eggs are unfertilized. If this happens, the honeycombs in the hive will look like cobblestone streets; this is sometimes called a lump colony. As a beekeeper, you must intervene if this happens (see page 97). The worker bee will perform many different tasks during her lifetime. Often, her age will determine her duties. Normally, she'll work inside the hive for the first three weeks, and then she'll get more assignments outside the hive as a draw bee.

The development from egg to finished bee—via larvae and chrysalis—takes twenty-one days. It's easy to recognize newborn bees as they wobble around on the honeycomb all tousled and with matted fur. After birth, the worker bee's first task is to perform as a preening bee. It has to clean itself and also clean out its own cell. The next three days, it will help cleaning out other cells where a bee has just hatched, making sure they are

After three weeks of different tasks inside the hive, it's time to start working on the field and collect pollen and nectar. After about two to three weeks, the wing muscles are worn out and the worker bee dies.

neat and tidy—the queen will only lay her eggs in clean cells. In the beginning, the brood gets fed honey and pollen by older bees, but already by the third day, they begin eating on their own and develop special glands that produce royal jelly, a vital and protein-rich secretion. After six days, the bee produces so much royal jelly that it's ready to become a feeder bee and start feeding larvae. After about ten days, the bee stops producing royal jelly and then it's time to leave the hive for the first time, both to defecate and to orient itself to its surroundings for future tasks. It will usually do this along with other young bees. On a warm spring day, you might spot a cluster of young bees hovering outside the hive—beekeepers call this the orientation flight. Note that this isn't the same as when bees swarm. Taking a closer look, you'll see that it's young bees moving in small circles with their heads directed at the hive. You can safely sit by the hive and study their flight training.

Now begins a new phase for the worker bee—a kind of transition from interior to exterior activities. It's time for nectar exchange. The task is to receive major air loads of nectar and pollen from its older comrades, the forage bees. This is extensive and hard work. The nectar has to be processed into honey, dried, and stored in wax cells. The pollen clumps that the forage bees have left in the cells have to be packed up and sealed with a drop of honey as food stores (called bee bread). A few weeks after birth, the worker bee's wax glands are fully developed and it can start working as a builder bee in the hive. If the colony needs more space, the builder bees make sure to build more wax cells, both so the queen has more room to lay eggs and so the colony gets more storage space for honey and pollen. The wax that the working bees use as building material comes from special glands on their abdomens. For a short time, the bees can also serve as undertakers and help clearing out dead bees from the hive. When the industrious and gentle attendants approach three weeks of age they have fully developed poison sacs.

The bee absorbs nectar or honey with a proboscis-like tongue that serves as a straw.

MOST WORKER BEES
LIVE FOR
4–6 WEEKS

ALL WORKER BEES
ARE
FEMALE

Some of them will now get a more defensive role, as guard bees by the entrance to the hive, for a few days. After the third week begins the toughest period in the worker bee's life—foraging. As a forage bee, it will collect nectar, pollen, propolis, and water. This is an extremely hard and arduous period that ends after about two to three weeks when the bee dies because its wing muscles have been worn out from foraging. The tasks of worker bees are not set in stone; rather, they depend on the colony's needs and where additional effort is needed. Some bees might skip certain tasks if they need to tend to more urgent matters in the hive. The colony might need more guard bees by the entrance to ward off thieving intruders or more help with the cleaning and construction of honeycomb, or the colony might grow so rapidly that more help is needed raising the brood.

The number of worker bees varies greatly during different seasons. During the winter, there are 15,000 to 20,000 bees in the colony. In spring and early summer there is a significant increase, which reaches its peak at the end of June, when the colony is at its biggest. If conditions are favorable, there may be as many as 60,000 to 80,000 bees in the hive. Subsequently, the colony diminishes in size as the queen lays fewer eggs, fewer bees are born, and many wear themselves out and die. The lifespan of a worker bee very much depends on when it is born. Bees born in early summer, during the intense work period, may only live four to six weeks; those born in late summer will survive the winter. Some can actually live until spring. That's almost seven months!

FROM EGG TO FINISHED BEE

After three days, the egg hatches a larva. For the first three days, it's fed protein-rich royal jelly by feeder bees. The larvae that will become queen are fed this jelly throughout the entire larval stage; the others will receive a mixture of small amounts of jelly and pollen. During the larval stage, the cells are sealed with a porous yellowish wax with pollen in it. The larvae grow rapidly and shed skin four times. They spin silk around themselves and become pupae. On the sixteenth, twenty-first, and twenty-fourth days, respectively, the fully developed bees begin to chew their way out.

Stages of development in bees in number of days

Queen	1 2 3 4 5 6 7 8 9 10 11 12 13 14 15 16	*Queen is born*
Worker bee	1 2 3 4 5 6 7 8 9 10 11 12 13 14 15 16 17 18 19 20 21	*Worker bee is born*
Drone	1 2 3 4 5 6 7 8 9 10 11 12 13 14 15 16 17 18 19 20 21 22 23 24	*Drone is born*
	Egg *Larva* *Pupa*	

THE BEES' PANTRY

To survive, bees need nutrients just like us, including proteins, vitamins, fat, carbohydrates, and minerals. All these are found in the pollen and the nectar they collect. Perhaps most importantly, they also need water. In the spring, water is the first thing bees are looking for; they need it to dissolve the sugar crystals in stored honey or in the winter food the beekeeper has given them. Water is also needed to produce bee bread for the brood. On warm summer days, the bees collect water and put small droplets of water on the honeycombs. As the water evaporates, the heat in the hive decreases.

Pollen provides energy for bees

Pollen is the plant propagation medium for flowers and conifers, but it is also the bees' main source of protein. Besides essential proteins, it contains vitamins , minerals and enzymes. Pollen has a different color, composition, and nutritional value depending on where it originates. When a bee visits a flower, grains of pollen stick to hairs on the bee's body. To make it easier to transport pollen to the hive, the bee's hind legs have shallow depressions with long, bent hairs along the edges, forming small pollen baskets (also called pollen pants). The bee combs up the light pollen grains with its legs, mixes them with nectar and saliva into sticky lumps, and packs them up in their pollen baskets. With a little luck, a really strong bee can carry a load of 0.0008 ounces (23 mg) of pollen.

Pollen

The need for pollen is especially great in spring and late summer, which is good to keep in mind if you're planning to put new plants in your garden. If you plant both early- and late-flowering plants containing lots of pollen, you're doing bees a great service.

The pollen collected by bees has a variable color spectrum, from light yellowish green to almost red. It's packed in cells and sealed with a drop of honey, which starts a fermentation process.

Great pollen-consumers

A regular-sized bee colony consumes between 55 to 110 pounds (25–50 kg) of pollen a year. Since each bee can carry only 0.0008 ounces (23 mg) of pollen in its pollen baskets, this means that the bees perform an average of 2.5 million to 5 million flights a year.

Harvesting pollen

Because of pollen's high nutritional value, many beekeepers harvest pollen in so-called pollen traps. Pollen can also be extracted from honeycombs with a special punching tool. Bee pollen is sold in health food stores. It contains all the beneficial ingredients of pollen and also has the antibacterial properties of honey.

Pollen basket

Flower nectar becomes honey

Bees need a lot of energy to perform their collection. They get their energy from flower nectar converted into honey. Nectar is a sweet, sugary liquid that acts as a carrier of nutrients in plants; it also attracts bees and other insects for flower pollination. The nectar is typically produced in special glands called nectaries and stored in nectar holds of the flower. Nectar should not be confused with honey. Nectar contains about 70 percent water and various kinds of sugars, mainly cane sugar (sucrose), but also fruit sugar (fructose) and dextrose (glucose). The sugar levels and the breakdown of different kinds of sugars vary between plants. The higher the sugar content in the nectar, the more honey that the bee can produce.

With its proboscis, the bee sucks up the nectar, which is then kept in the so-called honey stomach, also called the crop. The honey stomach can hold up to 0.002 ounces (57 mg) of nectar, which can be compared to the bee's own weight of 0.003 ounces (85 mg). A normal load, however, is 0.0005 to 0.001 ounces (14–28 mg). It takes more than a thousand flower visits to fill the stomach; this takes about an hour. In the honey stomach, the nectar's sucrose is converted into dextrose and fructose by mixing with the bee saliva, which contains a particular enzyme called invertase. This process starts on the way back from the flowers, and by the time the bee returns to the hive, it's time for nectar exchange. The forage bees regurgitate the nectar to the bees that work inside the hive. They, in turn, add more enzymes and after a while, they put it in the cells of the honeycombs.

The nectar has now been converted into honey, but it's not quite ready yet. First, it must be heated and ventilated to reduce its water content. By crowding together, the bees can raise the temperature in the hive. They can also fan their wings so that the water evaporates in the honey. When the water content has dropped from about 70 percent to between 18 and 20 percent, the bees seal the honey in the cells with a thin wax lid. For the

Honey storage

Some bee species are very frugal and store great surpluses of honey, while others are more wasteful and consume much of the nectar that is brought back to the hive immediately. The surplus is supposed to be stored for winter, but instead, the beekeeper harvests almost all the honey. To prevent the bees from starving to death during the winter, the beekeeper must provide the bees with sugar solution. The bees must collect lots of nectar to meet the colony's needs for honey. It's not unusual for a colony to consume between 110 and 220 pounds (50–100 kg) of honey in a season. The amount needed depends on conditions such as weather and temperature.

Bees have to collect lots of nectar to meet society's needs for honey. It is not uncommon that a hive consumes between 110 and 220 pounds (50–100 kg) of honey in a season. This amount is partly due to weather and temperature.

honey to be stored long term, and to prevent it from fermenting, its water content needs to be lower than 20 percent.

Honeydew for extra energy

Anyone who has walked through a tree avenue on a warm summer day has probably felt something sticky under their shoes. Long ago, people believed that honeydew fell from the sky and ended up on the leaves of plants. Today, we know that honeydew comes from aphids that suck sap from certain trees and excrete the excess in the form of droplets on their backs that end up as a sticky film on leaves and needles of plants. This sugary liquid essentially contains the same sugars as nectar: sucrose, fructose, and glucose. Bees suck up the honeydew, which is then treated in the same way as nectar. If the weather is warm and dry for a long time, bees get extra interested in honeydew. Honey that contains a lot of honeydew gets darker than normal because of its high mineral content. Honey made solely from honeydew is called forest honey and is more or less common from year to year.

Propolis, an antibiotic building material

When you open a hive to inspect it or harvest honey, you'll see that most parts in the hive are joined by a reddish-brown resinous material. It may even look like solidified droplets or long strings. This is propolis, a kind of resin that bees collect from trees and shrubs and use to repair and seal cracks or holes in their nest. Propolis comes from the resin of conifers and the sap on the buds of some deciduous trees. Hundreds of different substances in propolis have been found to have strong antibiotic properties that keep fungus and mold from growing in the hive. Propolis has long been used for medical purposes in Europe, Asia, and South America. It's a popular product in various health remedies and as an antibacterial agent in, for example, beeswax ointment.

You can harvest propolis by scraping it off the hive walls and frames. There are also special grids you can buy for harvesting propolis. Propolis has antiseptic properties that humans can take great advantage of.

DANCING COMMUNICATORS

Honeybees are efficient and frugal beings that focus on one type of flower at a time. When the nectar from one plant species is finished, they switch to the next one blooming. But how do all the bees know where the flowers are and how do they find their way back to the hive? The answer is that they communicate with each other through dancing. When a bee has found a good source of nutrition and filled its honey stomach, it returns to the hive. There, it spits it up a bit of nectar so others can determine its quality. Then, the bee begins to describe where the food source is by dancing on the honeycomb. If the nectar is in a location closer than 54 yards (49 m) from the hive, the bees communicates this quickly and simply by moving in a circle—the round dance. If it is further than 54 yards (49 m) away, the bee communicates this by performing the waggle dance and move in a pattern that looks like a flattened figure eight. The vertical line on the honeycomb corresponds to the direction of the sun. The angle [x] of the vertical line in the figure eight's centerline in the bee

The bee dance was discovered by the Austrian Karl von Frisch (1886–1982), a pioneer of ethology (the study of animal behavior). His research on how bees communicate was one of the reasons he was awarded the Nobel Prize in medicine in 1973.

dance indicates the direction to the food source in relation to the sun. The pace shows the distance. With the help of this ingenious dance, the bees avoid flying crisscross and aimlessly look for pollen and nectar. Instead, they can tell each other in a very precise way what kind of food source is available, where it is, and how far away it is.

Scents, tastes, and sounds

A bee can communicate and smell things using their two antennae. Each antenna has thousands of tiny receptors that can detect odors in stereo. In addition, it also has taste receptors on its legs. To a bee, wandering in complete darkness across the honeycomb entails a three-dimensional scent experience of the state of colony. Where is the Queen? Is she laying enough eggs? Are the food supplies full?

Anyone who has tried to catch a fly knows how good insects are at perceiving movements. The same goes for bees; they also have compound eyes and that's why you should move slowly and with small movements if you don't want to attract their attention. The bees have a wide field of view, but their vision is not particularly keen. They do however have an outstanding sense of color and can perceive nuances of, for example, ultraviolet light, which we perceive as white. They enjoy orienting themselves toward bright colors. Blue seems to be most popular, however, they have trouble distinguishing between black and red. Different colored hives will ease the orientation of bees. They can distinguish between right and left and between different geometric shapes and patterns. They can even recognize their beekeeper's face. Honeybees' hearing is nothing to brag about, but they can "hear" with organs that are very sensitive to vibrations. If the hive is exposed to sudden shock or impact, a couple of energetic bees will go to the entrance to see what's going on and possibly ward off intruders. Chickadees and other small birds use this to their advantage in the winter when they're hungry and have no food. They knock at the entrance of the hive to get the bees to appear, and then the birds will receive a meal.

CHAPTER THREE

YOUR OWN APIARY

Could beekeeping be something for you? Of course, you'll
need a sunny spot for the hives. You also need to be able
to check on the bees regularly during summer and
a few times in winter. Be prepared that it might take some
work and heavy lifting, but your effort will provide great
dividends. You get the privilege of nurturing probably
the world's most important insects; in return, they'll
give you a nice garden, as well as your own honey.

TIPS FOR THE ASPIRING BEEKEEPER

It's always good to meet with bees and beekeepers onsite to get a clear idea of what beekeeping is all about. Visit a beekeeper before you decide to get your own bees. If you don't know any personally, you can contact your local beekeepers' association.

Visiting a beekeeper can also give you a valuable connection for the future; it's great to have a mentor to consult for advice when starting out. Consider whether you actually have time to keep bees. Beekeeping isn't very time consuming, but you must be onsite regularly, especially in spring and summer.

If you're considering keeping bees, you could potentially ask a neighbor to look after them when you're not there. In early spring, you don't have to visit the apiary more than every three weeks, but in May to June when the colony starts growing quickly, you have to check on the bees more often—about every ten to fourteen days. Later in the summer, you can make less frequent visits. When autumn and winter arrives, you can take it easy, provided you've made sure the bees are ready for hibernation and that you've treated them against Varroa mites. If you can, it's also good to check on the hives a few times during the winter.

Joy shared is joy doubled

You might not be the only one in your area considering starting beekeeping. A shared apiary can become a natural gathering place and everyone can enjoy more flowers, larger fruit harvests, and self-produced honey. Together with someone else, you can invest in a few hives and maybe lease a small plot of land to set them up. Depending on where you live, why not set up a couple of hives in the courtyard of an apartment complex or outside a condominium, or on a rooftop or terrace? As a beginner, it can be good to have someone to share thoughts and investments with. If you're sharing the cost of a honey extractor, honey cart, and space to work with someone, you can reduce costs significantly.

A beehive can be a good gift for a gardening friend, but be prepared for shared custody. Bees are living creatures, and they need attention and care.

During holidays, it's also great to have someone to share the time it takes to look after the bees.

Another option is to start an apiary association, for example in a community garden where there's rich and varied flora. It may be time for more beehives in America's community gardens. If you decide to acquire your own hives, I recommend joining the American Beekeepers Federation. As a member, you'll belong to a local association where you'll meet others who can share their experiences and answer any questions you might have. You'll also receive information, offers, benefits, and newsletters where you can get lots of tips and advice. If you haven't already done so, signing up for a course on beekeeping is a good idea. A balanced mix of theory and practice is a great starting point for getting good at beekeeping. Remember that there are as many problems as there are solutions, so it might be worth it to listen to several different people, try different methods, and find what suits you.

Location

Where do you place an apiary? Keeping the hives close and accessible so you can check on and work with them easily is obviously good, but there are also other things to consider. The hives should be kept dry and protected from the wind, and you should avoid placing them in hollows where cold air tends to collect. The orientation of the hives is not very important as long as they get the right amount of sun and aren't pointing north, to avoid cold wind exposure. The bees also need a couple of yards of open space in front of the hives, preferably on your land. If you live in a densely populated area and it's difficult to find such a place, you can build a fence or plant a hedge a few yards in front of the hive. This gives the bees a steeper climb and they don't risk colliding with the neighbor mowing his lawn every week.

The location should be relatively calm, since heavy traffic noise, sudden shaking, and other disruptions adversely affect bee colonies. The hive should not be under trees where cones can fall onto its roof or branches can hit it during heavy winds. It's also not good if heavy loads of snow fall onto the roof of the hive.

A colony drinks lots of water, so you must ensure that the bees have ample access to clean water. This will reduce the risk of them gathering in your neighbor's pool. Even if you have streams or lakes nearby, it doesn't hurt to set out water sources in your garden, such as birdbaths. Just remember not to place them in front of the entrance cleat, where the bees exit. They often tend to defecate when they leave the hive and feces can spread disease if it ends up in their drinking water.

Obligations for Honeybee Health

Compared to some other countries, there are no national laws or regulations in the United States on bee diseases. However, the Honeybee Act, passed in 1922, restricted the importing of living adult honeybees into the United States. Regulations do, however, vary from state to state, based on the control of bee diseases. These laws regulate the movement of bees from place to place, apiary location and inspection, and treatment of diseased colonies. Check with your local state authorities to be sure you're following regulations properly.

Don't forget to talk to your neighbors!

Divine bees

In ancient times, bees had a high status in many cultures and were believed to be strongly connected to the sacred and the divine. Bees' behavior was considered prophetic. If a swarm landed on a house or a temple, it was seen as an omen or a blessing. Today, many people don't know have knowledge about the importance of bees and their behavior and become frightened and disturbed if they swarm.

Beehives don't take up much space, but the bees won't stay indoors or on your land all the time. If you live in the country and are a landowner, this usually isn't a problem; in an urban area, you should show consideration to your neighbors to avoid conflict. There are no clear rules about beekeeping in urban areas, but it might worry the neighbors; you should talk to them before establishing your hives. You can explain the importance of bees for the pollination of plants and the difference between bees and wasps. Most people are aware of the importance of bees after hearing alarming reports about global deaths of bees and other problems affecting honeybees. Some might be a little afraid of being stung; others may have heard about bees swarming and want to know more—often with a mixture of fear and fascination.

The risk of being stung is small but it does happen. Honeybees are gentle, peaceful beings with calm temperaments, but they do have a stinger, which they'll use if they feel threatened or need to defend the colony. Should you get stung, the stinger gets stuck in your skin along with the venom sac. Don't remove it with your fingers; more poison will be squeezed out. Instead, scrape the stinger off with a fingernail or credit card. The risk of being stung is great only if you root around in the colony without protective clothing, or pound on the hive and disturb the bees. In a garden, honeybees are rarely visible in places other than the blossoms of fruit trees or flowerbeds; they're interested only in collecting pollen and nectar. If you have hives nearby, you can be visited by a stray bee if you happen to have a jar of honey. Don't wave your arms around; just remove the jar. If there are several bees, simply move away slowly and carefully. They'll soon lose interest.

Sometimes, bees swarm. This is normal and part of their reproducing behavior. The queen bee leaves with about half the colony to find a new place to live, while those who remain in the hive raise a new queen. A swarm is an experience to witness and the humming black cloud looks more dangerous than it is. Before the bees swarm, they have filled their honey stomachs with honey so they're full and calm.

If you keep your distance, there's no danger and you can just enjoy the spectacle. After about half an hour, when the bees have settled in their typical clump formation, maybe hanging from a branch, you can take them down yourself (see page 115) or call a local beekeeper who will take care of the swarm. Whoever takes down the swarm usually gets to keep it. Remember, some people are allergic to bee and wasp stings. If you're beekeeping in an urban area, keep medicines handy to treat possible allergic reactions. If you or anyone else is stung by a bee or a wasp and have difficulty breathing, call emergency services immediately.

Honeybees are generally peaceful, but be sure to protect your eyes and mouth with a veil when you're working with the hive. When you feel more confident, you can work without gloves. It's quite a unique feeling to put your hands inside the hive and feel your small friends curiously walk up the back of your hand.

A few years ago, I discovered that I'm actually allergic to bee venom myself. Many times, I've been grateful that I was wearing a veil when I visited my hives, especially when the bees are a bit angry that I'm taking their honey. But a veil doesn't provide complete protection. Once, at the end of May, I was by the apiary to make a quick and simple inventory of the hives before I was going to town to meet some friends at the pub. I wore my overall with the veil but I used no smoke since it was just a quick visit.

The bees buzzed around me, but not any more than usual. At some point, I had to lift the veil. A curious bee came a little too close and got stuck in my mustache. When I gently tried to help the bee off my face, I felt a burning sensation on my lip. But the pain passed pretty quickly and I could continue my work without problems. When I returned to the house, I met my family, who had just come back from grocery shopping. They giggled and wondered what I'd been doing. Uncomprehending, I looked myself in the mirror. The bee, which I had forgotten all about, had stung me on the skin underneath my mustache. My lips were swelling evenly, and it looked as if I was sporting a perfect Hollywood mouth with the help of "Bee-tox". My pub visit had to be postponed and my wife laughed herself to tears for two days. I realized I'd had an allergic reaction and tests showed I was allergic to bee venom. I couldn't believe it—I'd just become a beekeeper!

A doctor told me that sensitivity to bee venom could be treated. For the past five years, I've received injections of bee venom equivalent to several bee stings every ten weeks. This will allegedly help my immune system not to react so strongly to bee venom. Is it working? I hope so. But if you happen to be extremely sensitive to bee venom, the chance that this treatment would work is unfortunately not very great.

HIVES, FRAMES, AND EQUIPMENT

The next step is to decide what kind of hives and equipment to buy. You can order catalogs from apiary suppliers or search the Internet. Reading about supplies can give you the impression that beekeeping is all about acquiring a lot of stuff. But as with so many activities, you really don't have to buy everything that's available. Just get the bare necessities and build from there.

In addition to the hives, you do need a veil, protective clothes, and a few tools for day to day hive management and for honey processing. I recommend you start with two hives, so that you have a backup. Then, it's up to you; once you've got more experience (and if you feel like you have the time) you may want to expand and acquire a many as ten hives or so. After a couple of seasons, you might even want to learn how to breed your own queens or immerse yourself in breeding bees, but then you're not a beginner anymore. The level of involvement and the size of your beekeeping is completely up to you—that's part of the charm.

Wooden or plastic hives?

To me, beekeeping an all-encompassing sensory experience where tastes, sounds, and touch are equally important to get the right feeling in the apiary; that's why I prefer wood hives. There are also so-called EPS hives made out of plastic (expanded polystyrene) that are cheaper, lighter, and easier to handle, but I don't think they are as beautiful as wood hives and I don't want them in my garden. However, if the bees happen to swarm, the plastic hives work well temporarily. A complete wood hive with drawers, frames, combs, and equipment for honey processing costs about $200 to $350. An EPS hive with the same equipment is significantly cheaper, about half that amount. If you're handy, it's relatively easy to build your own simple hives. You can find plans online or buy them from a beekeepers' association. Still, the most convenient thing is probably to buy what you need from an apiary supply store, which usually offers affordable starter kit for beginning beekeepers.

Straw hives

Thin sticks that bees can build vertical combs from are placed through straw hives. The hive often stands on a round wooden base and a wooden box.

Various models of hives

You've probably seen drawings of classic round hives made of straw on honey jar labels or in old children's books. For centuries, these were the most common hives in northwestern Europe. Straw hives are beautiful but not very practical, so today, they're used mostly as hives to catch swarms with or as decorative objects. I've inherited an old straw hive that belonged to my mother-in-law's grandfather, but so far, it's only been used as decoration in our home. Maybe I'll let the next colony that swarms live in straw hive so that I may experience what it was like to practice beekeeping in the old days.

About 150 years ago, three beekeepers, the Ukrainian Petro Prokopovych, the Pole Johann Dzierzon, and an American, L.L. Langstroth, independently discovered that beehives could be equipped with frames and honeycombs where the queen can lay eggs and honey can be stored. The revolutionized beekeeping in that one could now lift out the frames from the hive when they were filled with honey without destroying the bee colony. The frames were made square and thus, the hive also became square. The exterior then developed into the hive and the Langstroth hive. Today, there are also other, less common hive models. Most beehives that we use today have loose frames of wood or plastic inside one or several supers.

THE STACKING HIVE

The stacking hive is currently the most common type of hive construction. The name comes from stacking boxes on top of each other to increase the space. The hive consists of a base, a roof, and a number of boxes (brood chambers and supers) with frames. The brood chamber consists of two boxes. Each box usually holds ten frames. The base of a stacking hive can be screened, which provides good ventilation and makes it easier to examine the colony, but it's also fine to have a solid base.

Package kit

Example of a starter kit for a Langstroth hive

- 1 roof (lid)
- Molded boards / inner covers
- 4 drawers for brood chambers and supers
- 1 landing board
- 1 queen excluder
- 10 wooden frames
- 10 comb foundations

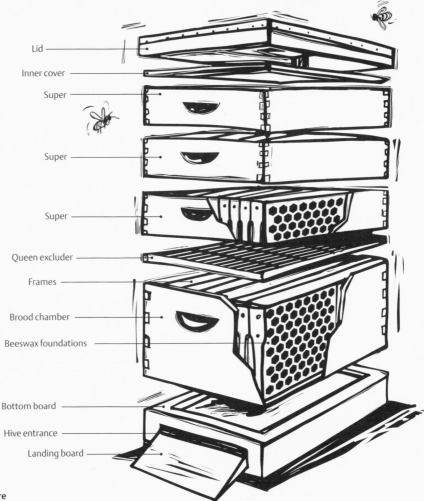

Lid

Inner cover

Super

Super

Super

Queen excluder

Frames

Brood chamber

Beeswax foundations

Bottom board

Hive entrance

Landing board

Stacking hive structure

Bottom board May be solid or screened.

Hive entrance The bees' way into the hive.

Landing board Landing space in front of the entrance.

Brood chamber The hive's heart and nursery. This may consist of one or several boxes of frames with combs, where the queen lays her eggs. In summer, the brood chamber can be expanded with more frames and possibly more boxes to make room for the queen to lay more eggs. The capped cells in the frame contain eggs, larvae, and pupae.

Queen excluder Placed between the brood chamber and supers to keep the queen from laying eggs among the honey. The excluder can also be used on the ground to prevent unwanted swarming.

Supers (one or more) placed on top of the brood chamber. The bees build wax cells and fill them with honey. Depending on the type, brood chambers and supers can look the same.

Frames These are square and consist of composite wood strips. They are inserted into both the brood chamber and supers. The frames hold the comb foundations.

Beeswax foundations These sheets of embossed wax are put into the frames. The bees then build wax cells on both sides of the partition wall in a perfect hexagon pattern.

Inner Covers Made in different materials, such as wood, glass, or plastic.

Lid Consists of a weather-resistant material such as sheet metal or tarpaper.

TROUGH HIVES IN SWEDEN

Trough hives aren't much seen in the U.S., but they were once common in other parts of the world, and are an interesting variation. The trough hive has a box structure with a removable rear wall, which makes it possible to increase the space of the brood chamber when needed. Uninsulated honey supers are placed on top of the brood chamber and are sheltered by an outer box structure. The brood chamber is expanded horizontally, in the front or in the back, with frames placed in succession. If the hive has a removable bottom board, it can easily be removed, which makes it easier to clean. Trough hives are well ventilated, but some may need extra insulation during the winter. Where they're used, they are great for beekeepers who want to learn more about how the colony works as it gradually expands, frame by frame, in spring and summer. I also think they are beautiful elements of a garden!

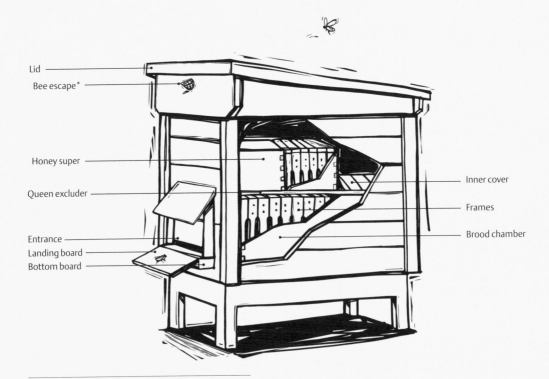

Lid
Bee escape*
Honey super
Queen excluder
Entrance
Landing board
Bottom board
Inner cover
Frames
Brood chamber

*This passage ensures that bees can get out but not back in.

FRAMES

Frames are available in various models and sizes, but there is no particular size that bees prefer and nothing to say that one kind is better than another. The most common frame model among noncommercial beekeepers in Sweden is called Low Normal (LN), while the one most commonly used worldwide is called Langstroth (L). Some models, such as Low Normal and Norwegian, can be used in both the brood chamber and honey supers. Others, like the Langstroth and Dadant, can use a larger size in the brood chamber and a smaller one in the honey supers to facilitate the work. In the end your priority is to avoid too much heavy lifting. The larger the frames, the heavier your work will be during honey harvest. A smaller frame format means lighter but also more supers to manage; a larger frame format means fewer but heavier supers. A honey super filled with honey can weigh between 90 and 110 pounds (41–50 kg), depending on the frame size and number. A low normal super full of honey weighs about 50 pounds (23 kg), while a full Langstroth super will weigh in at about 68 pounds (31 kg). The largest format, Dadant, can weigh over 110 pounds (50 kg)!

Honey frame type	Width (inches / cm)	Height (inches / cm)	Weight (pounds / kg)
Half-Low Normal Svea [HLS]	14.5 / 36.8	5.7 / 14.5	2.8 / 1.3
Low Normal [LN]	14.5 / 36.8	8.7 / 22.1	4.6 / 2.1
Norwegian [N]	14.5 / 36.8	10 / 25.4	5.5 / 2.5
Half Svea [HS]	12 / 30.5	5.7 / 14.5	2.4 / 1.1
Svea [S]	12 / 30.5	12 / 30.5	5 / 2.3
Farrar or ¾ Langstroth [F]	17.6 / 44.7	6.25 / 15.9	3.7 / 1.7
Langstroth [L]	17.6 / 44.7	9 / 22.9	5.9 / 2.7
Shallow, Low Langstroth, or ½ Dadant [LL]	17.6 / 44.7	5.4 / 13.7	3.3 / 1.5
Dadant [D]	17.6 / 44.7	11.25 / 28.6	7.2 / 3.3

The bees have begun to expand the frames of the walls with wax cells. The frames in the margin show the size variation between the different models.

Half-Low Normal Svea [HLS]

Low Normal [LN]

Norwegian [N]

half Svea [HS]

Svea [S]

Farrar [F]

Langstroth [L]

Shallow [LL]

Dadant [D]

THREADING THE FRAMES

Before putting the frames inside the hive, you thread thin metal wires through holes in the frame battens. Then you put the comb foundations in fitted frames purchased from a bee supply store. Use stainless steel wire for the frames—it lasts for several seasons and is easy to tighten if it starts to slacken. When the frames are threaded, I place the combs on the wire and heat them up with electricity from an old 12-volt car battery so that the wax melts and attaches—this only takes a second. If you heat it for too long, the wires will melt straight through the wax. You can also use a special generator (available from a bee supply store), but it's a bit more expensive. When you reuse your frames, you must first clear, scrape, and wash them.

THE WARM WAY OR THE COLD WAY

When I bought my first stacking hive with low, normal frames, I was a little befuddled trying to figure out the direction of the frames. A Low Normal frame has a square base, which means that the frames can either hang parallel or angled to the entrance cleat. My trough hive didn't cause the same conundrum; with it, the brood chambers decided the direction of the frames. If you place the frames parallel to the entrance cleat, it's called warm dwelling or cross building. If you place them in an angle, it's called cold dwelling or length building. There are divided opinions about whether one way is preferable over the other. Mainly, it's about personal taste and choice and above all about what kind of frames the hives can hold. To the bees, it probably doesn't matter.

Threading frames is a pleasant winter craft but sometimes when your apiary grows unexpectedly and quickly, you may need to make more frames even during summer.

Natural beekeeping

In recent years, some old hive construction and beekeeping methods have been dusted off and reintroduced in many parts of the world. Unlike conventional beekeeping, where frames are used in the hives, the bees are allowed to build their wax combs freely. This is called natural beekeeping, which is quite paradoxical since humans have designed all these models of bees' nests – even though the bees can build their honeycombs any way they want. Simplicity was the intention when Abbé Warré designed his frameless hive in the early 1900s. The Warré hive, or "People's Hive," has boxes in the same size with top slats for the bees' own comb building and an insulation box on top. If you're interested in the Warré hive, there are books that describe methods and drawings; you can also download information from the Internet.

The top bar hive (TBH) is another, very simple hive model that is used a lot in Africa and comes in many different designs. Similar models were probably used in early beekeeping in Europe. The hive has become popular in the United States and Britain, but isn't common in the Nordic countrie and parts of Europe. The top bar hive is a horizontal hive, but instead of using frames, wide slats are used. One major difference from conventional hives is that the bees build freestanding honeycombs from a narrow track in the middle of each slat. Since the slates merge to form a watertight roof, there is no need for cover boards. The hive looks like a long trough on legs, with sloping walls. In Africa, the top bar hive is hung some distance from the ground to protect it from pests.

Additional equipment

In addition to hives and frames, you need a few more pieces of equipment, but as a beginner, you shouldn't acquire anything more that the essentials. With time, you'll know what you need. It might look professional to wear overalls, but a jacket and jeans can also suffice. Be sure however to protect eyes, throat, and mouth with a veil (and maybe a hat for shade). You can manage the bees without gloves most of the time, but as a beginner, it's best to keep your gloves on. In addition to this you'll need a hive tool, a bee brush, and a beehive smoker. Some beekeeping suppliers offer affordable equipment packages that contain the basic necessary equipment for beginners. When you begin to approach the year's first harvest, you'll need basic equipment for honey processing. An uncapping fork is crucial and an uncapping tray is good to have but an old roasting pan can also suffice. You'll need a regular strainer and a fine mesh sieve, available in various styles, and also a large honey container. A honey extractor is a large and expensive investment; a used one might be a good option. I managed without one my first year by cutting out the combs, placing them in jars, and letting the honey slowly drain out of the wax cells. I also tried squeezing the honeycombs in an old fruit press and it worked fine. Sharing an extractor with other beekeepers is another option. Finally, you'll need jars, lids, and maybe also some labels. An uncapping fork and sieves are often included if you buy a complete hive package.

Work equipment

- Jacket and pants
- Veil
- Gloves
- Hive tool
- Smoker
- Bee brush

Basic equipment for honey processing

- Uncapping fork or knife
- Honey strainers
- Large honey vessel
- Jars with lids

BEWARE OF SECOND HAND

If you're a beginner, I would advise you to not buy used equipment (except for the extractor). Without specific knowledge of various bee diseases and how you should sanitize the equipment, there's a great risk that you make a failed investment that costs both time and money and might also squash your newly discovered enthusiasm for beekeeping. Buy new equipment so you won't have to worry and can sleep well at night. If you're taking over an active apiary with existing equipment, it's a good idea to let a beekeeping expert inspect the colonies before you buy and possibly move them.

Moving permission

All the equipment, like supers and frames, should be inspected and have a moving permit if they are to be moved across a parish boundary in an infectious area. This also applies to the bees.

FINALLY TIME FOR THE BEES!

When you've put your hives out, acquired all the equipment necessary, and prepared the frames, there's only one thing missing: the bees. We mainly have four kinds of honeybees: Nordic bees, ligustica bees (Italian bees), carnica bees (krainer bees), and buckfast bees. What kind will you choose? To make it easy, you can either consult a bee supply store or go to the website of American Federation of Beekeepers and look up contacts in your local Beekeeper's Association. They'll know what kind of bees most beekeepers in your neighborhood have. If you're lucky, you may even get a hold of someone who has one or more new colonies to sell. If that's not possible, your local beekeeper's association can guide you further. A colony costs between $250 and $400. In many areas, beekeepers like to try to keep the particular breed of bees as "pure" as possible in order to preserve each species' different, distinctive, and positive characteristics, whether they're frugal, gentle, not prone to swarming, fast-growing, or good hibernators. It does happen that queens and drones of different breeds mate. This creates a kind of "local mix," but is usually not a problem. If you're unlucky, bees can at worst lose their positive disposition and get aggressive, which you naturally want to avoid. If that should happen, you'll buy a new fertilized queen from a queen grower with calm bees that are not prone to swarming.

Ligustica bee

Buckfast bee

Carnica bee

Nordic bee

Dark European honeybees

(*Apis mellifera mellifera*) are dark, almost black in color, and have been in Scandinavia for thousands of years. They're well adapted to the climate and work intensively over the short summers. They are relatively prone to swarming and are susceptible to certain diseases. The Dark Honeybee has become a generalized species in Europe with local names such as Nordic honeybee, English honeybee, German honeybee, etc. In some parts the species is endangered, and preservation projects were created to support it. Today, you can find them all over northern Europe.

Ligustica honeybees

(*Apis mellifera ligustica*) also called yellow Italian honeybees, are yellowish-brown in color. They're adapted to the Mediterranean climate with mild, wet winters and long, dry summers. The breed is popular, especially in the south. They hibernate in large colonies, are considered good nectar collectors, and can provide great honey harvests even when the nectar season is short.

Carnica honeybees

(*Apis mellifera carnica*) are grayish brown in color. They descended from the mountain regions in the Balkans and have been adapted to that climate: long harsh winters, short springs, and hot summers. They also do very well in our climate. Colonies are small in the winter but grow very rapidly in the spring and can effectively make use of early flowering plants. Their rapid expansion rate makes them quite prone to swarming.

Buckfast honeybees

(*Apis mellifera*) vary in color, often brownish and resembling the Ligustica bee. They originate from the monastery Buckfastleigh in Devon, England. To eradicate a disease epidemic in the early 1900s, Brother Adam began experimenting with crosses between domestic English bees and Ligustica bees. They are a popular bee type, hard working, frugal, not prone to swarming, and disease-resistant.

Purchase and install the colony

Moving hives

When the bees are out flying, they learn to recognize the area and always return to the place where the hive stands. If you move your hive to the other side of the garden during summer, a large number of bees will fly back to the original place and pile themselves up there. If you have to move the hive, you can do it two yards forward or backward without major problems, or one yard sideways over a period of a few days. Alternatively, you can move the hive three miles (about 5 km) away, let it stand there for a few months, and then return it to a new location in your garden. Then the colony has new bees with no relationship to the old, original hive location.

You will likely purchase bees in advance of setting up the colony; the beekeeper or seller will let you know when you can pick them up. Your apiary should be at least three miles (about 5 km) from the original hive so the bees don't return to it. Beehives with colonies should be transported early in the morning or in the evening, when bees are inside the hive. If you're buying colonies for two hives, you'll need a car with lots of space for base and ceiling. Don't forget veil, gloves, and straps to secure the hives.

It's easiest to transport bees in EPS hives. You can either borrow transportation hives from the beekeeper and move the colonies to your hives when it is convenient or leave your own empty hives with the seller in advance and collect them with the bees in place later. You can often leave empty frames with wax foundations in exchange for frames with bees that you purchase. Make sure that base and lid are firmly closed so no bees escape and secure the hives with straps so they don't tip over. Close up the entrance cleat with a piece of foam or fabric, but make sure the bees get enough air, especially if it's hot in the car. When you get home, place your hives in their permanent location, or lift the frames from the shipping hives into your own hives. This is important because it's difficult to move the hives later. Don't open the hive entrance wider than two inches (5 cm), or the bees might not be able to defend themselves against intruders.

THE QUEEN'S PAINT MARK

The queen's color indicates the last number of her birth year

- 🔴 0 and 5
- ⚪ 1 and 6
- ⚪ 2 and 7
- 🔵 3 and 8
- 🔴 4 and 9

When you purchase a colony (or just a queen), the queen can be color coded to show what year she was born. This makes it easier to know when it's time to replace her. If the color fades and needs touching up, or if you're marking a new queen, you can do it yourself with color you get from the bee supply store. Carefully lift up the queen, mark her, and put her back.

I was advised to buy carnica bees when I started beekeeping. They've been calm and easy to care for and given me great honey harvests. The queen is often color marked when you buy her. This queen was born in 2012.

CHAPTER FOUR

BEEKEEPING YEAR-ROUND

The beekeeping year begins when you're preparing your bees
for the long winter when no food is to be found in nature.
On the other hand, it's in spring when everything comes to life
that you can start working with your bees again after a long
break. Since the seasons vary in different parts of the world,
it's difficult to specify exactly when various tasks should be
performed. But bees know what to do. Your job is
to listen to them and give them optimal conditions for
a good life both in and outside the hive.

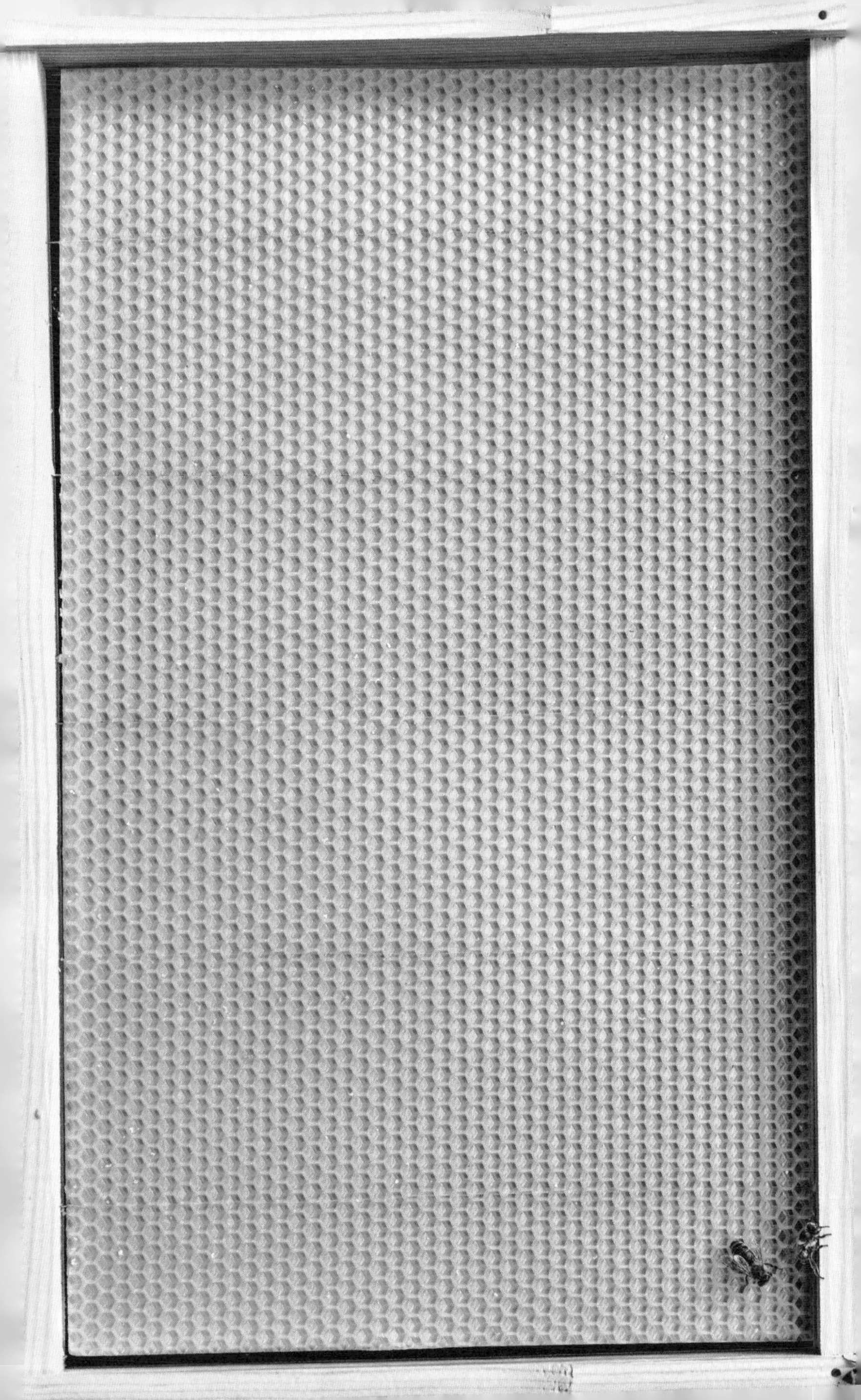

SPRING TASKS

One sunny day, when everything has begun to warm up, the bees leave the hive for the first flight of the year. This is called the cleansing flight and it is the beginning of the bees' spring development. After being cooped up in the hive throughout the long winter, the bees need to defecate. Bees are cleanly creatures and prefer to defecate outside of the hive. One can understand the relief they might experience now that they can defecate, often collectively. If there's still snow on the ground, you can see brownish, yellow dots in front of the hive. The performance should be viewed at a distance, as bee feces are very difficult to remove. It's very important to not disturb the bees before the cleansing flight is completed, otherwise they might defecate inside the hive. So even though they've begun to move around and leave the hive, wait a little before you make your first visit.

Feed control

During winter, the bees gather up close to each other in a formation called a winter globe. They move slowly between the center and outer edges of the globe to maintain the temperature between 77 and 86 °F (25–30° C) in the middle, where the queen sits. The worker bees take turns to sit on the outside where it's colder. The colder it is outside, the more food the bees need to maintain high heat in the globe. When it gets warmer outside, the bees begin to move more, and then they also need more food. However, if the colony has at least 40 pounds (18 kg) of sugar solution at hibernation preparation in late summer, everything should be in order. After the clearing flight, it's time to ensure that the bees have enough to eat in their food storage. There should be at least two frames of food left. Lift the roof, put your hand on the cover boards, feel the warmth of the bees' activity, and hear the muffled buzzing of thousands of bees moving in the darkness of the hive. Carefully remove one or two of the rear cover boards. If there's food left in the hive, you'll find it in the frames at the ends.

The beekeeper's notebook

It's good to keep notes about your visit to the apiary. You should, for example, write down:

- date
- time of day
- temperature
- weather conditions
- status of the colony
- what procedures you have performed with the hive

Supplemental feed

Boil water and some sugar. Allow the sugar solution to cool slightly. If the feed is lukewarm, it's easier for the bees to pull it down quickly in the hive. Use an inverted jar with a lid that you've perforated with small, drilled holes (0.03 to 0.07 inches (0.76–1.78 mm) and place it over the feeding hole, which is usually found in the middle of the cover board. You can also pour the sugar solution into a feed balloon that has a feed cup on a feed board (see page 156). There's also special feed dough you can buy.

Hopefully, a few early spring plants have now begun to show, so the bees have the opportunity to find some pollen and a little nectar. If there are not two full frames with food in the hive, you probably haven't been generous enough at hibernation time. I've actually experienced that a hive perished despite food remaining on the edges of the hive. If very cold weather hits, the bees need their food close to the winter globe. If it's too far away, they risk freezing to death on their way there, and the colony starves to death. To be on the safe side, I've therefore sometimes provided support food in the form of lukewarm sugar solution in early spring. One advantage of having stacking hives is that with a little experience, you can get an idea of how much food remains by lifting the hive and "sensing" its weight. If it has a glass or Plexiglas cover, you can easily see if the colony moves and there's food remaining.

BASE CLEANING

The next procedure you need to perform is cleaning the base of the hives. Choose a nice but cool day when the bees are not out flying. The cleaning is quite simple and relatively quick, but you have to be meticulous, especially if you move the bases between colonies. You can do this task on your own but, the first few times, it's easier if you get help from another person. At this time of year, the stacking hive usually consists of one or two boxes (brood chambers) on a base. Carefully lift the box and place it on a clean surface next to you, or on top of an extra base, if you have one. Never place the box directly on the ground. The hygiene in the hive is important, so the bees shouldn't come in contact with soil or dirt unnecessarily.

While cleaning, you should dispose of any dead bees the hive has not already taken care of. Collect dead bees from the floor of the hive in a bee-tight bag and discard. The colony doesn't tolerate dead bees and are good at cleaning the hive, but there are still often some poor wretches remaining in the corners and it doesn't hurt if you help to remove them. It doesn't need to be a disaster if you find a lot of dead bees. As long as there aren't droves of thousands of dead bees on the ground, you don't have to worry about the colony's health.

The next step is to scrape the base clean as much as possible and wash it with mild soap and warm water. Rinse and dry it before you put it back and return the hive to its place. Bases made of wood can be scorched with a propane blowtorch or hot air gun. Scorch it until the surface of the wood begins to change color. Trough hives with removeable bottom boards are easier to clean than stacking hives. Just pull out the bottom board to do the same procedure and then put it back again. If you are short on time or don't want to disturb the bees more than necessary, the cleaning can wait until it's time for the big spring inspection.

You can check that the bees have eaten by pulling out the bottom board and see how much wax residue that's fallen down when they chewed up the winter feed. If there's little residue on the ground not enough food has been consumed for some reason; if there's a lot, you might need to provide extra.

The colony evolves

The spring sun begins to feel warmer and at this point, you've probably seen a lot of activity around the hives. When the bees begin to move, they need to replenish their dwindling food supplies. You might be burning with curiosity to check the colony, but resist the urge. Instead, sit down by the hives and enjoy the gentle hum and the sight of bees coming in for a landing at the entrance with big clumps of yellow pollen on their legs. During spring, there may be a shortage of food in the wild, and there's still a risk of cold snaps.

If a cold period occurs, the bees' need for energy increases, but the cold also prevents them from flying out to look for food. There's a reason why April has sometimes been called the bee-killing month. Inside the hive, the colony has begun to grow as the queen lays thousands of eggs next to each other in the wax cell's frames in what's called a brood globe. For the brood development to be most efficient, the temperature in the brood globe should be kept at a constant 93 to 95 °F (33.9–35° C), which requires a lot of energy from nectar or honey.

LOOTING

The availability of food is limited in nature during early spring and it's difficult for bees to accumulate a surplus of food. A large and strong colony that develops rapidly in the spring is in desperate need of readily available food sources. If there's a weak colony nearby that has a large food supply, it may become the target of looting. The weak colony isn't strong enough to fend off the robbers, loses all its food stores, and is quickly doomed. This is called looting. If you see intense traffic at the entrance cleat in a colony you know is a little weaker, you must take action. Reduce the hive entrance to about 1 inch (2.5 cm) so the colony can defend itself. If the looting continues and you have access to a place at least three miles (4.8 km) away, move the hive so the looting bees can't find it. Move the hive in the evening, when all the bees are inside. You can return the hive to its original place after forty days.

The great spring inspection

Is everything okay in the hive?

1. Check food stores—is there still enough food?

2. Check the number of bees—are there plenty of bees on the frames and do they seem to be in good health?

3. Check the queen—does the colony seem to have a healthy queen?

4. Check the brood—are there eggs, larvae, and capped brood?

5. Check for disease—any signs of infectious diseases?

At last! The real spring warmth is finally here. A sunny and warm day in April, or perhaps as late as the first week of May, the temperature rises to 50 or 55 degrees °F (10–12° C). Now it's time for a proper spring inspection of the hives. It's a great feeling to finally get to stick your hands in the hive, feel the warmth of the bees, and sense the sweet smell of wax. But one should, as always, not disturb the bees more than necessary. Try to work quickly and methodically, so the colony doesn't get chilled. The first few times, your spring inspection will take a little while, but once you grasp all the elements, it shouldn't take more than five minutes. The bees tend to be quite gentle this early in the spring, but as a beginner you should put on your veil and gloves. However, take it easy with the smoker; that's better for both you and the bees.

First, lift the lid and the cover boards to see how the bees have managed during winter. Does the colony seem healthy? Begin by removing the box from the base of the hive. If your hive is comprised of two boxes, remove and check them one at a time. Never place the boxes directly on the ground. Then, lift one frame at a time from the box and try to estimate the amount of bees—is it crawling with bees, and can you find an egg-laying queen? Don't worry if you have trouble finding her. If there are eggs and larvae in different stages as well as capped larvae—in other words, larvae in cells covered with gently domed lids—it means there should also be a queen. If everything seems to be as it should be and if there's winter feed remaining in the frames, you'll know that bees have fared well. If there are several frames with food left in them, you can lift one out and possibly move it to a colony that is short on food or save it. It may be needed if you decide to expand your apiary and grow a new colony. Try to distribute the frames with food between your colonies so the availability of food is roughly the same in all the hives. But keep in mind that there's a risk of infection! Only move the frames of your colonies if they are healthy. If a colony is lacking a queen,

Sometimes, it can be difficult to locate the queen. If you can see eggs in the cells, it means she's there, but if you want to be sure she lays fertilized eggs, you also have to find capped brood.

Lump colony

If you find frames with cells that curve sharply outwards, like domes, it has developed a lump colony. This is a sign that the queen has run out of sperm and is only laying unfertilized eggs. It could also mean that the worker bees have begun to lay eggs. Such a colony has no future. One solution would be to merge it with another colony that has a fertilized queen.

eggs, and larvae, you can merge the two colonies. Set the box with the colony without the queen on top of a box of a different colony with a newspaper in between. First, make a few cuts through the paper with the uncapping knife. Then, the bees will smell each other and you don't risk that the merger goes too fast and there'll be a fight.

Lift up one frame at a time and make sure everything looks good. Because the eggs are unfertilized in a lump colony, only drones can develop.

What is Varroa?

Varroa mites are considered the most serious pest problem for honeybees worldwide. These small parasites attach between the rear body segments of the bees and weaken them. In addition, they spread viral illnesses that can cause entire colonies to collapse. Varroa mites reproduce by laying eggs in the cells; when the mites hatch, they feed on the brood. A colony can provide a full harvest of honey despite being attacked by mites, but the colony collapses later in winter. Therefore, it's important to treat colonies against mites in batches to ensure their health before winter.

Varroa Sensitive Hygiene

VSH is a behavior trait of honeybees to detect and remove the pupae that are infested with fertile female varroa. VSH activity is inherited and results in significant resistance to mites.

DISEASES AND PARASITES IN THE COLONY

If you discover that your colony has deposited a lot of excrement that looks like spots on the combs, base, and walls inside the hive, it may have become infected by the intestinal parasite *Nosema apis* or *Nosema ceranae*. These parasites make it difficult for the bees to absorb proteins, which makes them weak.

In order to make a diagnosis, samples need be analyzed under a microscope. Large spots need not be *Nosema*. They can also appear because the bees have eaten autumn honey, which is hard to digest, or that they've become stressed or disturbed by something and therefore defecated inside the hive. If it turns out that the colony is infected you may need to euthanize it, depending on how widespread the infection is, because *Nosema* is very contagious. Set aside the infected frames and treat them with white vinegar along with other frames later in the fall and the winter.

Now is your chance to see if the colony has been infected by Varroa mites and if so, to what extent. Pull out the base and inspect what you find there. The mites look like miniscule, brownish-red shells. You can't do anything about the mites this early in the season, but you get a picture of the colony's health and know you'll have to treat it later (see page 106). Place all the debris in a paper bag and burn it, or destroy it in some other way. This reduces the risk of spreading diseases.

In addition to *Nosema* and the Varroa mite, which both spread diseases, there are other, less common contagious bee diseases, such as American foulbrood. If you suspect that your colony is diseased and you're unsure of the cause, contact a local bee representative and ask for help. If it turns out that your bees are infected with a contagious disease, it's important that the right actions are taken. It's better to call one time too many than not at all.

Brownish yellow spots on the bottom of the hive don't necessarily mean that your colony is doomed. The bees may have eaten autumn honey, which is hard to digest, or become disturbed by something and therefore defecated inside the hive.

The bee in the middle of the picture has a reddish brown, 0.08-inch (2-mm) varroa mite on its body. If the bee had been as large as a human, the size of the mite would correspond to that of a bunny.

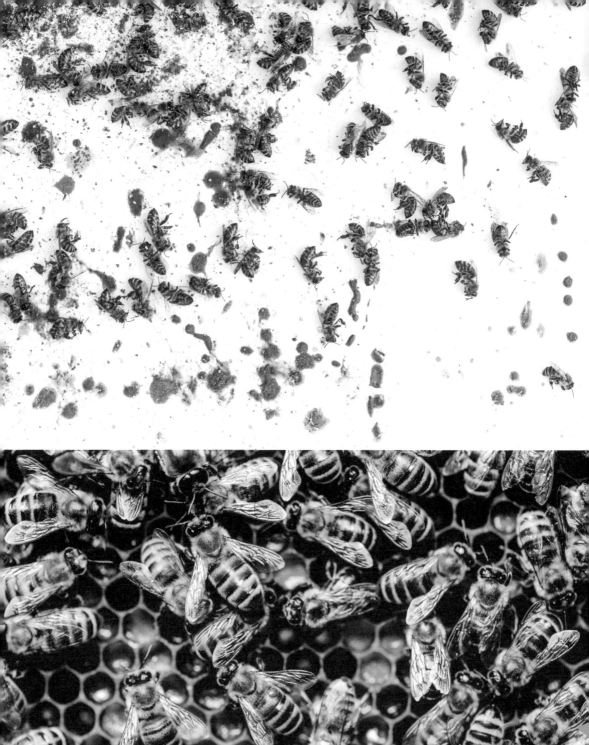

Beekeepers often walk around puffing

You might know or have seen beekeepers puff smoke into the beehive. When smoke enters the hive, the bees think it's burning and prepare to leave and find a new home by crawling down between the frames and filling their bellies with honey. When the bees are full and contented, they get calm and not very prone to sting. Usually, honeybees won't sting, but if you rummage around with the frames with careless movements, they get disturbed. They also don't like sudden shocks. Therefore, always work with gentle movements so the bees hardly notice you're there. Never work with the hive if you've been drinking alcohol. Like many other animals, bees dislike the smell of alcohol and other strong scents, such as perfume, aftershave, garlic, and many other smells.

The smoker is used to produce cool smoke, which doesn't harm the bees. For fuel, use a natural material that burns without a flame and also produces a lot of smoke. In well-stocked bee supply stores, you can buy wood pellets or burlap strips specifically made for bee smokers. You can also use peat blocks cut into appropriate sizes; these can be purchased in most garden stores. If you think these are unnecessarily expensive, you can use virgin pine cones, which are found for free in nature.

You can light the smoker with, for example, newspaper, wood shavings, or tar sticks. Sometimes it's hard to get it started—the heating material can be a little damp or in other ways difficult to ignite. When ordinary matchsticks are not enough, I usually use a heat gun or propane torch. These have the advantage of working in all sorts of weather. Never use synthetic materials or toxic solvents when using the smoker. When they burn, they form very toxic gases that are dangerous for both bees and humans and also end up in the honey.

Ignite the smoker a little while before going to the hives. For fuel, use natural materials that emit a lot of smoke without producing a flame—never use synthetic materials or toxic solvents.

EARLY SUMMER CHORES

As a beginner, you learn a lot by looking down into the hives. Following a hive at close range during a whole season, during different weather conditions, is a great way to gain knowledge about how the colony functions. It's only when you go through the colony and inspect the frames in the brood room that you can find out what that needs to be done. Try to be a little ahead of the bees and plan your visits, taking into consideration the weather and how flowers and plants develop.

In the past, beekeepers kept track of when different plants and flowers bloomed to determine when it was time to perform various chores in the apiary. In early spring, you might only need a few visits to the apiary, but now in May and June, you should visit it about every ten to fourteen days.

The growth of the colony varies greatly during the year. In the winter, the colony is at its weakest with between 15,000 and 20,000 individuals. In July, it's at its greatest, with 80,000 bees. The different bee speicies also develop differently over the year in terms of the number of individuals. The colony of the dark European honeybee develops slowly in the spring and has a relatively small number of bees in the summer, but a large number in winter. Ligustica bees have a great number of bees in winter and summer and a fairly even growth during spring. On the other hand, Carnica bee colonies have a strong growth in the spring, a large number of bees in summer, and a small number during winter. If you have Carnica bees, it's therefore important to be extra observant in early summer and expand the beehive as the colony grows. If you don't keep up with it, there's a great risk the bees will swarm.

Expand the colony

When the bees have become so numerous that they almost fill up the brood chamber, it's time to give the queen more room for her eggs. If you have a trough hive, place a few expanded frames (frames where the bees have built wax cells on the partition wall) in front of the brood cluster and a few frames directly behind. As a beginner, you may not have a lot of expanded frames, but it works just as well with frames that you added wax foundations to. If you have a stacking hive, you'll expand the colony by placing a box with nicely expanded frames on top of the box where the bees lived during winter.

Equalize the colonies

In early summer, colonies develop rapidly and the number of bees increases drastically. If you have several colonies and notice that one of them is not growing like the others, it may be worthwhile to equalize the number of bees. This will probably also yield more honey. If the colony isn't expanding, it might be because it is diseased, so to avoid cross-contamination, make sure to check it carefully before changing anything. You can mix bees freely between different colonies without conflict, so move a couple of frames with covered brood from the strongest colony and place it in the weakest, next to the other brood frames. Choose frames with lots of bees where you can see young bees about to crawl out. Replace the frames you moved with expanded frames that have only wax foundations. If you should notice that one of your colonies have an explosive development, equalization can also reduce the risk of the bees swarming.

If you notice bees crawling on all visible frames when you open the hive, it's time to add a box of empty frames to give the colony more space to grow. If a colony develops very quickly or lags behind you may need to move frames with bees and covered brood between the hives. But first, make sure the colonies are healthy.

Fight against Varroa with drone frames

While expanding the brood chamber in your colony, it's also time to do something about the Varroa mites. Since the nectar that will become honey is on its way to the hive in the next few weeks, there are not many options when it comes to fighting the Varroa mites. A simple, non-toxic method is to use drone frames. A drone frame is an empty frame without wire with a wax partition wall that can be divided into two or three compartments. If the bees are free to build in empty spaces anywhere, they usually build drone cells at this time of year. Varroa females prefer to lay their eggs in drone cells; when the eggs hatch, they feed on the drone brood, which is either injured or dies. By removing and destroying covered drone brood, you're effectively combating the spread of Varroa.

The empty drone frame is labeled clearly and placed next to the brood cluster. The bees will expand an equal amount of wax in all compartments. If the frame is divided into two compartments, take it out after ten days, cut out the expanded wax in the second compartment, leave the wax in the first compartment, and put the frame back in the hive. You can save the wax you've removed and melt it down, or throw it away.

After another ten days, the bees have covered the drone cells in the first compartment and expanded the second compartment with new wax cells. Cut out the first compartment with the covered drone cells and put the frame back in the hive again. Put the wax cells you've removed in a labeled plastic bag and keep it in the freezer for at least two hours before you put them in the trash or feed birds with it in the winter. If you're curious, you can break the wax up and study the mites before you throw away the frozen cells. Repeat this process until there's no more drone brood in the cells. If you have split the frame in three parts, cut out two compartments after seven days, and thereafter a tray at a time every seven days. This also gives you reason to regularly visit the hive.

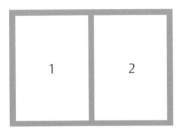

Place an empty drone frame next to the brood chamber.

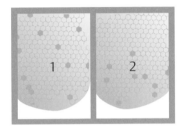

After 10 days ...

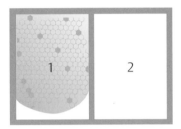

... cut out the expanded wax in the second compartment.

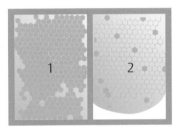

After 20 days ...

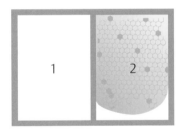

... cut out the covered drone cells in the first compartment.

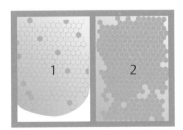

After 30 days ...

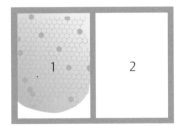

... cut out the covered drone cells in the second compartment again.

Time to add the honey supers

The beekeeper's prime season, or honey season as it's also called, extends from when the dandelion and rapeseed blossoms until the heather is in bloom. When this occurs varies depending on the weather and area of the world, but it's usually around the beginning of May to the end of August. This is when nature really explodes with blooming pollen and nectar; the bees can collect food and accumulate a surplus of honey. For the bees to get more storage space for the pollen and honey, you must put the honey supers in place. When the first honey super is more than half full with bees, it's time for the next one. Place the new super under the old. If you have a trough hive, move the first honey super to the back and place the new honey super in the front. One advantage of the trough hive is that you can use honey supers with fewer frames; this makes the work easier.

Sometimes it can be difficult to judge when it's time to add the first honey super. A rule of thumb is that the time is right when the brood chamber's two supers are filled with bees, brood, pollen, and honey. I usually put it in place when the air has become warmer and dandelions and cherry trees blossom. It's important that you don't add the honey super too early since the number of bees in the hive decreases in early spring. Then, the old winter bees will die faster than new bees have time to be born. If there are not enough bees that can build cells for the queen's egg-laying, the colony will stop growing.

Carefully lift the lid and inner covers to check the amount of bees in the hive. You don't have to use the smoker—it will only bother the bees. To make sure the queen doesn't enter the honey super and lays eggs there, place a queen excluder between the brood chamber and the honey super. The grid is wide enough so that the worker bees, which are much smaller than the queen, are still able to crawl up and down between the supers. If the

bees have placed a lot of honey mixed with eggs and brood in the partition frames of the brood chamber, you can take an uncapping fork and carefully cut holes in the wax lids—if you do this, the bees will move the honey to the honey super.

Bear in mind that a queen excluder is not always a guarantee. One year, I had the misfortune of getting a young queen that was so skinny that she managed to crawl through the excluder. When it was time to harvest the honey, the whole hive was filled with frames containing both brood and honey. We didn't harvest much that year. A good alternative for those who are going away for two or three weeks is to put several honey supers in place, with newspaper in between as insulation. When the first super is full, the bees will chew through the paper and continue to fill the next. But before you start using this method, you should find out what the nectar supply is like in the area and know that your bees aren't prone to swarming. This is not a method for beginners.

Some beekeepers believe that a queen excluder reduces the honey harvest, but there is no scientific evidence for this.

Throne change – replacing your queen

For the bee colony to thrive and develop, it needs a healthy and fertile queen. Replacing a queen can be done in two ways. Either the bees will do it or the beekeeper will. The bees do it by swarming or if they are unhappy with her because she's old, worn out, and not laying enough eggs. Queen replacement without swarming is called quiet shift. The colony will pull out a pair of cells and hatch a new young queen, which mates and begins laying eggs. The old queen is left in the hive for a while before the bees eventually attack and throw her out. Bees can also raise a new queen if the old one has disappeared because you accidentally squeezed her to death or if you lost her in the grass when you moved frames.

As a beekeeper, you should replace the queen if your bees are angry and you get stung a lot when you visit the hive or if you feel that your hive swarms all the time. You can try raising a queen yourself, but it's easier to buy a fertilized one from a breeder. They keep good track of their queens' genes.

Preferably, you should purchase a queen from a breeder in your area, but if there isn't one nearby, you can order one from a breeder further away and get her sent in the mail. Look for ads on the Internet or in your bee association newsletter. You can switch to a fertilized queen anytime during the season, it's easiest to add the new queen when the bees are hibernating and you are dividing your colonies. (see page 120). The queen is delivered in a small travel cage; its exit is sealed with a plug of sugar (or candy cork). Remove the outer seal and hang the cage between two brood frames. It takes enough time for the bees to nibble through the sugar for the colony to accept the new queen's pheromones.

Before releasing the new ruler, make sure you find the old queen and remove her. If you don't, you're taking the risk that the new queen won't be accepted and is killed by the colony. Then you'll have to start the whole process over.

If you discover that your bees have built lots of cells to supersede the queen, it's best to split up the colony by making a division (see page 120).

Swarming

Swarming is the colony's natural way to procreate, but as a beekeeper you want to avoid it because half your colony may disappear and the honey harvest will be smaller. If your apiary is in or close to a residential area or a town, your neighbors might not appreciate if the swarm ends up in their chimney or on their deck roof. The risk that a colony will swarm is greatest from mid-May to mid-July.

A hive strives for balance. When the queen starts egg production in the spring, she needs a lot of space for the eggs. If she doesn't have empty cells to put them in or if her egg laying decreases for other reasons, her pheromone production drops. Working bees detect this imbalance and prepare to divide the colony by starting to build queen cells. Order won't be restored until the colony has swarmed and a new queen is in place. While the young queens develop, the worker bees put the old queen on a diet so she can regain her flying ability. She is then forced out of the hive with about half of the bee colony. The worker bees fill their honey stomachs with honey and take off in a big swarm to gather in the typical cluster shape, big as a football, usually under a branch near the apiary. From there, scouts are sent out to search for a new place to live. They've usually been out for several days in advance and searched the terrain for suitable cavities like hollow trees, chimneys, or the like. Now, the entire swarm lifts and the journey continues toward the new settlement, which could be located several miles (approximately 5 km) away.

Remaining in the hive is half of the old colony, which consists of worker bees, some drones, and a number of queen cells from which new queens soon emerge. Usually, the first-born queen kills her rivals before they hatch. If there are several young queens in the hive at the same time, the colony may form several swarms. There are also other reasons why bees swarm. Some colonies may for instance develop an affinity for swarming. Another reason is that in early spring, the colony produces many young bees that become idle and feel the need to start a new colony.

CATCHING SWARMING BEES

You have to catch the swarm before it has the chance to take off for the new settlement. If you're unsure of how to do this, don't hesitate to contact someone with more experience in your local beekeepers' association or a swarming expert.

If a swarm has settled in a chimney or house wall, consult with experienced beekeepers. To the extent that it's possible, it's better to take care of the swarm and allow it to live rather than killing the bees. But sometimes, there's unfortunately no other option.

Put on protective clothing and veil: Even if the bees are fed and calm, it's foolish to take unnecessary risks. You'll need a bucket or large cardboard box, a queen excluder, a bee brush, a smoker, and an empty hive. If the swarm is hanging from a branch, shake the branch firmly so that the bees fall into the box. Use the bee brush if necessary. If you have tall trees in your apiary, you may want to invest in a long ladder. The important thing is that you get the queen into the box; then the rest of the bees will follow.

Place the queen excluder over the box so the queen can't get out and bees that didn't come along have the opportunity to join the swarm. Put the box in a dark place, or in a shady spot, and leave it there until evening. Meanwhile, prepare the empty hive with a number of extended frames or frames with partition walls, depending on the size of the swarm.

In the evening, it's time to let the bees move into their new home. Put a board or panel in front of the entrance to the hive and shake out the bee swarm onto it. Give the bees a little puff of smoke, and they'll get moving. It's quite impressive to see the new colony following their queen, all marching in the same direction up the board and into the hive. After about fifteen minutes, the swarm board is usually empty. If you want to make sure the swarm won't take off again, place a queen excluder in front of the entrance of under the brood chamber.

After a couple of days, remove the queen excluder and insert two frames, one with mostly honey and one with mostly pollen. When you catch a swarm and don't replace the queen, her swarm-prone genes will live on. To prevent this, you'll remove the old queen and replace her with a new, fertilized queen.

It was the beginning of June and our entire family was ready to leave for my brother's birthday party when we heard a strange and loud roar. Since we live fairly close to an airport, my first thought was that the planes were flying very low that day. But when we looked out into the garden, we saw a dark, high pillar rising thirty feet (10 m) into the air. "Oh no, don't let them swarm now! We'll be late to the party." I had to step into my overalls and put on the veil. The whole family watched, fascinated by the spectacle. This time I was lucky, because the swarm began to settle on the hive, but I didn't understand why the bees behaved the way they did. I called my mentor, who explained that for some reason, the queen had not come along with the swarm. She could be hurt and lie somewhere on the lawn in front of the hive.

"If you find her, you'll have to kill her. The bees will select a new queen."

In that moment, I heard my nine-year-old daughter shouting from the garden that she'd found the queen. What were the odds that she'd recognize and find the queen on 270 square feet (26 sq m) of overgrown lawn? But she did it! As the colony didn't have a queen, it would return to the hive. The danger was past and we could leave for the party, half an hour late.

Another time, we were on our way to the coast for the weekend, to celebrate our oldest daughter's birthday. Everything was going great until a neighbor called and told me they were having a kids' birthday party in their garden. "However," he said, "we have a little problem…there is a humming black cloud over our patio where we have set the table."

Being on the other side of the country when your bees are swarming isn't great. Thanks to my neighbor, who was calm and curious about the bee swarm, I had time to contact a swarming emergency service which arrived quite quickly. The swarm seemed to attract the interest of several people in the neighborhood and I received continuous updates with photos via text messages. With the help of a long ladder, the swarm was brought down from the tall tree where it had settled, and the kids' party could continue, almost as if nothing had happened. Not all neighbors are that easygoing and reasonable.

REDUCE THE RISK OF SWARMING

In the past, when straw hives were used as apiaries, beekeepers actually favored early swarming. In his book, *The Self-sufficient Life and How to Live It*, John Seymour mentions the expression: "A swarm in May is worth a load of hay; a swarm in June is worth a silver spoon; but a swarm in July is not worth a fly." Today, we're trying to avoid swarming. As a beginner, it's especially disappointing if your new hobby suddenly takes off for the woods. If you find one or more queen cells that seem to be ready, you can be pretty sure that the colony wants to swarm. Drone frames are good places to start looking. Another sign of swarm preparation may be that there are no eggs in the frames or that the queen has slimmed down. It takes some experience to discover these signs.

I have sometimes used the queen excluder to prevent swarms when I have gone away for shorter periods during the summer. When placed between the bottom and the brood chambers, the queen cannot get out. But even if it's practical, you risk a young queen being stuck inside the hive and killing the old queen. Then, you've ruined a nice colony. It's not great to have to clear the queen excluder of drones that have become trapped, stuck, and met a painful death.

If you're a beginner, it's easy to worry the bees will swarm and you may wonder if you can go away at all during the summer. From the very start, my mentor said to me: "The risk that the bees will swarm is at its greatest until July 10; after that, you can take some much needed time off." It's not quite this set in stone; you can probably go away for a weekend or a few days in June as well. But, before leaving, make an inventory of your hives and be sure that the queen has space for laying eggs, and that there are no queen cells. If you do this and some other swarm preventative measures, you can go away for a few days in good conscience.

In the beginning, I thought it would be enough to remove all the queen cells I found, but the bees still wanted to swarm. You can delay swarming and you can pull out the queen cells, but that still won't reduce the bees' inclination to swarm. The best way to prevent that is to divide the colony.

SWARM PREVENTION MEASURES

Increased space

The most important thing is to ensure that the queen has plenty of room to lay her eggs. If she walks on the outer frames, it's a sign of overcrowding and that means that the colony's impulse to swarm can be triggered. To create more space for egg laying, you can, while adding honey supers, remove a few frames with honey and replace them with empty frames with wax partition walls. You can also expand the brood chamber with an extra box of expanded frames under the queen excluder.

Clipped wings

Many queen breeders deliver their queens with their wings clipped. It sounds worse than it is—they just cut off a small piece of one wing tip. When such a queen tries to fly with the swarm, she ends up on the ground a few feet in front of the entrance to the hive. Usually, a cluster of bees gather where she is and you can find her easily. When the rest of the swarm notices that the queen is not with them, they'll return to the hive.

Queen trap

If you need to go away for a few days during the most intense swarm period, you can put a queen trap by the entrance to the hive. A queen trap is a grid with sufficiently large gaps to let worker bees through, but not the queen. Never use a queen trap (or a bottom queen excluder, see page 118) for a longer period; instead, find, a bee sitter who can look after the hives instead. Don't forget to check the colony when you return from your trip.

Switching to a breed of swarm reluctant bees

If you notice that your bees swarm easily, I recommend that you buy a new queen with genes that are swarm reluctant or simply switch your entire colony to one that is reluctant to swarm.

Expand your apiary by dividing it

In nature, the bee colony grows by dividing itself. If you notice the bees starting to build queen cells and are about to swarm, or if you want to expand your apiary with more colonies, you can create a division.

You simply start a new colony. This can be done from mid-May to late July. The division can be done in different ways and with different kinds of equipment, but it should contain a queen, young bees, brood frames, frames with food, and an occasional empty frame. The number of brood frames you'll need depends on when in the season you make the division—the later, the more frames with brood you'll need. More food is also needed. The new colony has to grow strong before hibernation. My homemade trough hive has a side exit in the rear of the longer side, which I can temporarily open to create a division. If you have a stacking hive, you can create the division by using a box that you place on top of the hive or in a new location. You can

either use a smaller division box with five frames, a regular, large insulated box which you fill in with foam, or partition with a separation wall on a division bottom that has the entrance in the opposite direction (available from bee supply stores). If you perform the division in June or July, you'll need to use the whole box. If I have several strong colonies, I usually pick frames and bees from two to three different ones so I'm not weakening only one. I locate the old queen so she doesn't get included when I move the frames. If I choose to let the bees raise a queen themselves in the new colony, the brood frames that I take to the new hive have to contain eggs and larvae that are no more than a day-and-a-half old. I select two nice looking brood frames with lots of bees, eggs, and larvae on it. Then, I take two more frames with lots of bees; one should be heavy with food and the other should contain quite a lot of pollen. The fifth frame is an empty frame with a wax partition wall or expanded wax cells.

I place the brood frames in the middle of the new box so the bees can easily keep warm, with the honey and pollen frames on the side. I fill in the box with, for example, a piece of foam, put a lid on the box, and reduce the entrance to a maximum of 2 inches (5 cm). After a week, I remove all the queen cells on the brood frames except for one, which will develop into a new, strong queen. There should be a lot of bees on the frames. If there's a shortage of bees, I shake down some more from other colonies before I put the lid back on. If the weather gets a little cooler, I can give them some extra sugar solution. Now, I let the divided colony rest for two weeks.

When a new queen has hatched, she will mate and begin laying eggs so a new, strong colony starts growing. It takes about a month for the bees to raise a new queen themselves. If you want to get your divided colony going a little faster, you can insert a frame with a finished queen cell or order a fertilized queen from a breeder. When she is delivered, remove the seal on the transport cage before you hang it between the brood frames.

May

July

◇ Brood frame
◇ Honey frame
◇ Pollen frame
◇ Empty frame

The principle when making a division is to place the brood frames in the center, with pollen- and honey frames around them. The later in the season, the more frames you'll need.

Don't be too eager

You must be careful when lifting the frames in and out. If a queen cell has been built so that it is secured in the two frames, you may accidentally tear it out if you're too eager. It's better to wait until the queen has hatched.

If you choose to buy a fertilized queen for your divided colony, your colony will be established faster than if you let the bees raise a queen on their own.

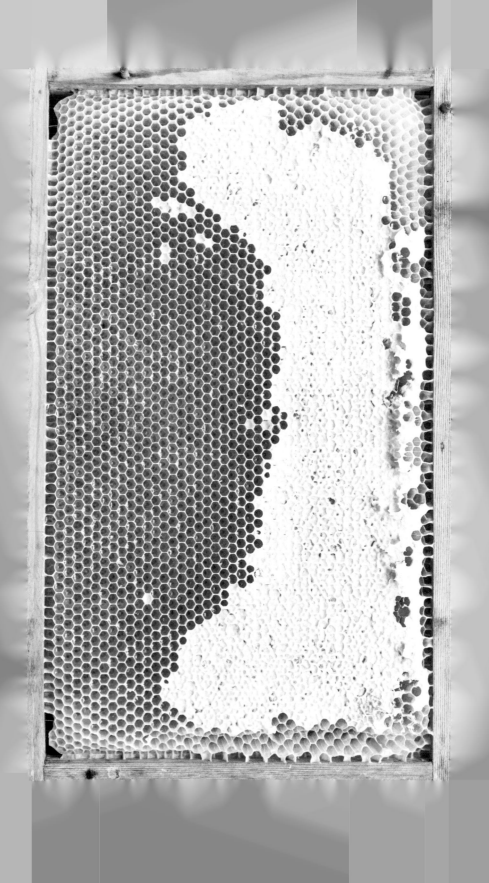

THINGS TO DO AT THE PEAK OF SUMMER

Throughout June, the bee colony expands exponentially and reaches its peak in early July when there's an abundance of pollen and nectar. In two months, a strong colony can increase from 15,000 to 80,000 bees. And then comes the reward for all your labor with the bees: At the end of June, you can usually do the first honey harvest. It feels wonderful to go down to the hives and lift out the first frames of covered honeycombs filled with yellow gold. Until mid-July, or as long as the queen is productive and lays a lot of eggs, the risk that the bees will swarm is still great. Make sure the colony has plenty of room, go through the brood chamber thoroughly, and look for signs of possible swarm preparations. If you find an occasional queen cell, tear it out. If you find many, I recommend that you take additional swarm preventative measures (see pages 118–119).

Varroa control—again

Hopefully, the method of using drone frames to prevent against Varroa that you did earlier in the season has been effective. But the mites usually don't disappear entirely, so sometime in the second half of June, you should check your hives again. Do this by counting the daily fallout of mites in the hives. Stacking hives usually have a special Varroa bottom. If you have a regular bottom or a trough hive, you can use a special Varroa insert that you slide in under the brood frames. Divide the number of dead mites by the number of days the inset has been in the hive. One mite a day represents about 120 mites in the colony. If you find five or more mites per day, you should do a short-term treatment with formic acid in the middle of August for the colony to have a chance to survive the winter (read how to do this on page 152). If you find ten or more mites per day, you have to start the short-term treatment with formic acid as soon as possible, but no later than in July. The honey should always be harvested beforehand.

Honey harvest

During the height of summer, you'll need to make sure that the bees have enough storage space for all the honey they collect at all times. Therefore, you should gradually add more honey supers. As soon as the top super is more than half full of bees, I put on a new super directly on top of the queen excluder. If the summer offers an endless flow of nectar, it's better to harvest honey several times than to build skyscrapers of honey supers. I usually harvest two to three times: the first time in the middle of June and the last time during the second half of August. You can also harvest a little at a time throughout the summer. If you want, you can harvest according to different flowering times and get different types of honey. But it can be a little time consuming and works best if you know which plants bloom when and where. If it's a dry summer, don't forget to set out water sources in the garden. The nectar contains a lot of water that the bees must evaporate by fanning it before the honey is ready for storage. To assure that the honey won't ferment, the water level has to be below 20%. When the bees have sealed all the honey cells with a thin wax lid, the honey is ripe and ready to harvest.

You can take all the honey frames that are completely covered and the honey frames that are only half covered. With some luck, you can take whole honey supers without having to pick and choose among the frames. You can easily test if the honey is ripe by shaking the frame. If liquid is splashing out, put it back into the hive. When you harvest in early summer, you shouldn't move honey frames from the brood chamber. The honeybees need it so that brood production won't be disrupted if there is a spell of cooler weather. The bees born in late summer and fall are the ones most capable of handling hibernation the best and, therefore, they are particularly valuable.

The supply of nectar is greatest during the height of summer and the bees are working hard. Make sure to continuously expand the hives with more honey supers so they have space to store all the honey.

PREPARATIONS

Mind the hygiene

Remember that honey is food. Never place honey frames directly on the ground as there is bacteria in and on soil that can leave spores in the honey. Use the smoker sparingly, because the smoke can also leave particles in the honey.

Honey harvesting is always done on a warm and sunny midday when most of the bees are out flying around. Put on your veil and covering clothes. It's good to light the smoker well in advance of visiting the hives because it can take a while to get it going. You'll need a bee brush, a hive tool, and honey supers with empty, expanded frames. Bring as many honey supers as you think you need—I prefer to bring too many rather than too few—since you are replacing the full honey supers with more supers with empty frames. As a beginner, you usually won't have expanded frames, but it works really well using frames with partitions—the bees quickly expand them at this time of year. The harvesting is heavy and your working posture can be challenging, so make sure you have a good raised surface next to your hives on which you can comfortably work. You should also have a trolley that you can unload the honey supers onto. Alternatively, you can drive your car up to the hives if possible.

EMPTYING THE HIVE OF BEES

Before harvesting the honey, you must empty the hives of bees. Three methods are commonly used: a bee emptying bottom (along with latch grid), bee blower, or a bee brush. A bee escape board is a disc in the same shape as the honey super with edge strips and one-way exits that the bees can leave through, but not enter again. Place the bee escape board under the honey supers you are harvesting honey from. When the bees leave the boxes, they can't get back in again. There are several models, some better than others. If the bee escape board works as it should, the harvest will work quickly and smoothly. Some beekeepers use a bee blower. They angle the honey super at 90 degrees and blow through it so that the bees are blown away rather than flying away on their own. It's probably an effective method, but it seems rather noisy. I do not want to use this method; I'd rather

harvest by hand with a little frame shaking and bee brushing. It's contemplative work that makes me feel I'm present in the here and now. I let go of any other things I might have on my mind and become completely focused on what I do.

HARVESTING

Before I begin harvesting, I gently lift the cover boards to check how many bees are in the hive. This is when I use the beekeeper's most important tool: the hive tool. Cover boards, boxes, and frames can be stuck and difficult to remove because the bees have sealed the hive with propolis and wax. I insert the hive tool into a crack and wiggle it gently until things come loose. If bees fly up right away, I give them one or two more puffs of smoke; this will make them crawl down between the frames. Now I can lift up a few frames and figure out how much honey is covered.

On a raised surface next to the hive, I've put an empty honey super with a wooden board as a lid. I lift one full honey frame at a time and shake the bees off over the honey super with a sharp jerk. The bees that refuse to let go of the honey, I brush off gently before I put down the frame in the box next to it and put on the lid. You have to be quick to close things up so that zealous forager bees won't try to take it back. It doesn't matter if one or two bees manage to crawl into the box.

I then continue until the new box is filled with honey frames. I fill up the empty honey super with empty expanded frames or frames with wax partitions. If I'm extracting the honey right away, I return the emptied frames to the honey supers. If you have several hives, just continue until you are finished. Naturally, you don't have to harvest all the honey at the same time—you can do as you wish. Harvesting is fairly time-consuming and intense, but the reward is the wonderful feeling of having the year's first honey harvest.

Handling the honey

Equipment for honey processing

As a beginner, you don't need everything I've listed here, but you cannot manage without an uncapping fork and sieves.

- Uncapping fork, roller, or knife
- Uncapping tray (or roasting pan)
- Honey sieves; one with coarse mesh and one with fine mesh
- Stirrer
- Large honey vessel (110 lb / 5 kg) with tap
- Honey vessel (66 lb / 30 kg)
- Jars with lids
- Honey extractor

If you don't have time to extract the honey immediately after harvesting, you can temporarily store it for up to a week, depending on honey type and the room temperature. Store the honey frames in a space where bees cannot get in, such as a shed. Honey frames should never be stored in cold and damp places, such as a basement. Most importantly, the room in which you extract the honey should be easy to keep clean and dust free, and the bees have to be kept outside. If you use the kitchen, don't cook at the same time. If you're planning to sell the honey and not just use it for yourself, make sure that you find out what rules apply to commercial food handling and hygiene. You can buy the most necessary equipment in a bee supply store.

Over time, you'll discover what you need to simplify some steps in the process. I think the experience of honey as a natural product is intensified when you scrape it directly from the honeycomb or if you cput a piece of honeycomb in an empty glass jar that will then slowly fill up with fresh honey. I have a strong childhood memory of when I visited my older sister during summer break: I always got cut a piece of honeycomb to dip into the evening tea. The honey melted and I chewed on the wax for a long time, pretending it was chewing gum. As a beginner beekeeper, I stood in the kitchen using a juicer and honey strainers to extract the honey. I still use our kitchen for the uncapping, extracting, straining, and filling, with messy consequences that aren't always so popular with the rest of the family. Despite this, everyone gets involved in honey processing and it has become one of the highlights of the summer.

My average honey harvest usually end up being 77 to 88 pounds (35–40 kg) per colony. One year, I got a significantly smaller harvest because of a swarm and two divisions, which in turn yielded a bumper crop the following season, when I ended up harvesting 175 pounds (79.4 kg) of honey from one colony.

Uncapping forks are available in various models and materials; they work well and don't cost a lot. There are other uncapping tools that are also good but a bit more expensive, such as uncapping rollers and uncapping knives. The latter are also available as electrically heated luxury versions.

UNCAPPING

Before you extracting, you have to remove the wax lids, which the bees have placed over the cells, from the honey frames. The easiest way to do this is to use an uncapping fork over a roasting pan or an uncapping tray. Don't uncap more frames than you'll extract from. When I'm about to uncap the honey, I place the honey frames in a special stainless holder that is standing on a plastic crate. It's slightly tilted so that the uncapped honey can drip into a coarse strainer at the bottom of the crate. I remove the thin layer of wax with the fork and then I place the frame in the extractor. The wax that sticks to fork, I scrape down into the sieve where the honey gets to drain. The bees are very careful with their gold, and I'm the same—I gather every drop. I clean the wax and melt it so I can use it in ointments later.

The water content in honey

With a simple refractometer, which costs around $60, you can measure the water content of the honey. It should be below 20 percent before you extracting. If it contains a lot of water, it may be good to dehumidify it in a warm place (preferably above 86 °F / 30 °C). In addition, it's easier to extract the honey if it's warm.

EXTRACTING

To get the honey from the honeycombs, you'll use a honey extractor. It looks and works much like a centrifuge. There are motorized extractors as well as simpler, hand-cranked versions. You put in a number of full honey frames and start cranking. In the beginning, it may be a little difficult to find the right speed, but you'll soon learn. The honey is thrown out of the frames along with a little wax residue. It runs down and the sides of the extractor and gathers at the bottom. From there, you pour it through a tap. During my second year as a beekeeper, I found a cheap hand-cranked stainless extractor with room for four frames. It's easy to move and clean, and I still use it. When you buy an extractor, it's important that it's made of a stainless material and easy to clean.

Four uncovered honey frames are in place in the extractor when I start cranking. The frames spin faster and faster. The only sound you can hear is a little creaking from the crank handle and a whooshing sound from the extractor drum's interior. When I've reached a steady speed, I lift the lid a little bit to listen. I smell the sweet scent and hear the first drops of honey hitting the extractor's walls. It sounds just like a gentle summer rain. Then I know I've found the right speed.

STRAINING

Before you can start to pour the honey in jars, you have it to strain it from wax residue, pollen, and maybe an occasional dead bee. Obviously, there are strainers in various models and materials. You need two sizes, one with coarser mesh and one with a finer mesh; you should place the coarse strainer inside the fine strainer. Many strainers stand on three legs and if you're using one of these, you must be careful so it doesn't fall over when you pour in the honey. The honey vessel must be covered while you're performing the straining to make sure dust and other particles don't come in contact with the honey. It's not pleasant to find debris in the honey when you open a jar. There's something very special about newly extracted honey and it's especially healthy at this time, full of important lactic acid bacteria. I keep the wax remaining in the strainer; later, I melt it down and make beeswax ointment of it. Then, I put the lid on the honey vessel and let it stand at room temperature for a day.

SKIMMING

One day after I've strained the honey, a white foam forms on the surface. This is wax particles and bits of pollen residue. To get rid of the debris, I put a sheet of waxed paper or plastic wrap on the surface and press out all the air bubbles. Then, I pull away the sheet so that the wax foam and a little honey that has gotten stuck on it are pulled off. Quick and easy, and almost all the foam is gone! I usually squeeze out the wax paper or plastic wrap and collect the pollen honey (in other words, the leftovers). This cloudy and protein-rich honey, I keep for myself.

The honey flows pretty quickly through the screen. It's tempting to insert a jar under the flow and get completely fresh, newly extracted honey for your summer lunch.

BEWARE OF CRYSTALS

I and many others have longed for the first honey harvest of the year. Demand is high and therefore I want to pour the honey into jars as soon as possible. The color and the flavor vary from year to year and tend to be very aromatic, with flavors from all the flowers of the surrounding gardens. I like the early summer honey just as it is—untouched, raw, and runny—but if you're not planning to eat or give away most of it, and want to store it for the winter, it should be stirred or seeded. Almost all honey solidifies after some time and if you don't stir or graft it, it will solidify into large crystals and acquire a coarse texture. Stirring or grafting helps set the honey with a finer texture as it crystallizes.

STIRRING

Stirring is started the day after straining. The honey should be kept cool, at about 57 °F (13.9° C), throughout the entire stirring process. Stirring the honey requires patience. It's difficult to say exactly how long it will take, but it will take about one week to over a month, depending on the type of flower nectar the honey is made of. Stirring 110 pounds (50 kg) of honey is hard work. In the bee supply store there are agitators for manual or mechanical stirring (the latter will be mounted in a heavy drill and used at low speed). Every morning and evening, you stir the honey slowly for about five minutes. You then repeat the procedure until the honey gets cloudy and the agitator can stand upright on its own in the honey without falling sideways. Only then is it time to pour it into jars. If you stop the stirring too soon, the honey will become too hard. If you stir it for too long, it may get too loose. Experienced beekeepers know exactly when to stop.

SEEDING

To avoid having to stir the honey like a maniac, you could opt for seeding; this saves a lot of time and effort. Grafting is a way to accelerate the crystallization process and it's the method that

I use. I mix a seeding batch according to the prescription in the margin, and then I mix the seed into an equal amount of newly extracted honey. After this, I slowly pour the mixture into the large vessel with the rest of the honey harvest. The honey has to be stirred throughout the entire process.

When the honey is thoroughly colored by the seeding, it's ready. It mixes more easily in room temperature. After a day or so, when all the air bubbles are gone, it's time to pour the honey into jars. Afterward, when you then set the jars in a cool place (50 to 57 °F / 10–13.9 °C), the crystallization goes faster and the honey takes on a nice creamed consistency. After about three weeks, the honey is light and firm, but smooth as butter.

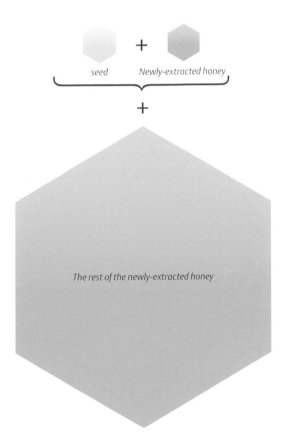

seed   Newly-extracted honey

The rest of the newly-extracted honey

Making seed honey

There are many different recipes for seeds on the Internet, but this is what I usually do:

1. Weigh the newly extracted honey and keep it at room temperature.

2. To make things easy, let's assume that we have 100 pounds (45.5 kg) of honey. Take 3 percent (3 pounds / 1.4 kg) of the honey and pour it into a bowl with a lid. Add finely crystallized honey (your own or purchased—the nicer the better) so that it represents 10 percent of the contents of the bowl = 0.3 pounds (0.14 kg).

3. Stir well for one or two minutes, until the mixture has a uniform color and texture.

4. Place the seed in the fridge.

5. Gently stir the creamed seeding for about thirty seconds, morning and evening (it must not get warm) for about three days. The time can vary depending on the water content of the honey.

6. The inoculum is ready when its consistency is firm but not hard. Let it stand for an additional day.

7. Enjoy your fresh, nutritious honey!

POURING

When you've stirred or grafted the honey, immediately pour it into smaller jars— you don't want it sitting with a single giant pot. Honey jars are available from the bee supply store in a variety of designs and sizes in either glass or plastic. Choose what suits you. I prefer hexagonal glass jars that can hold 8 or 16 ounces (237 or 473 ml). The hexagon shape is sleek and space saving, but the jars are a little more expensive. I begin by weighing the entire honey harvest—if I haven't done it before—in order to calculate the number of jars I need. During the pouring, I use a digital kitchen scale, which I put on a tray under the tap. I then place an empty jar on the scale to avoid a lot of mess, reset the scale, and pour the honey. Then I know I have the right amount of honey in the jars. When all the jars are filled and sealed, I scrape out the honey vessel with a rubber spatula to the very last drops. The kids get to lick the spatula.

Then it's time for the icing on the cake: the labels. There are self-adhesive sheets you can buy in the stationary store so you can make your own labels. Finally, I put the honey jars in the cool (50 to 57 °F / 10–14° C), dark pantry. If you intend to sell your honey to local shops, first check what rules apply for produce hygiene. If you're a member of a Beekeepers' Association, you can order standard labels with personal EAN codes.

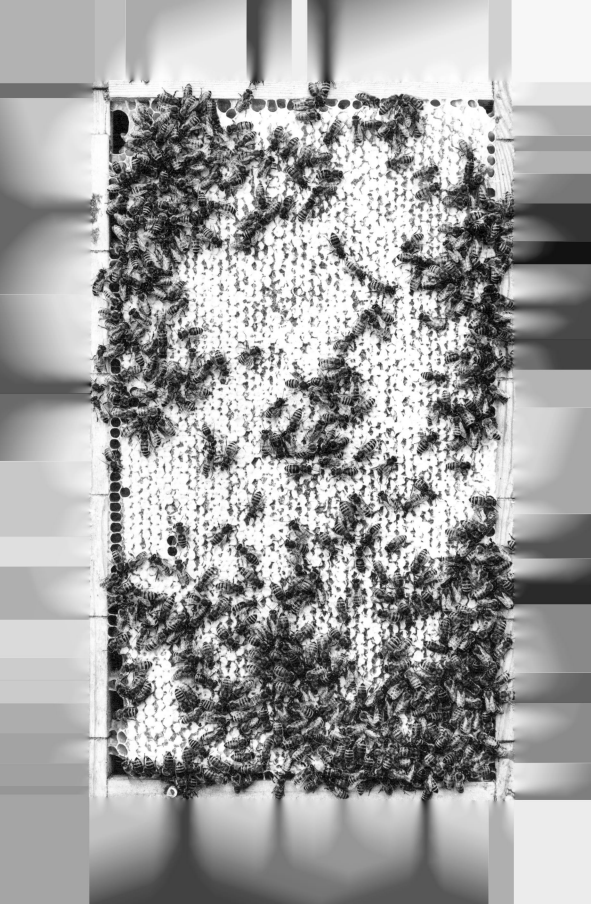

LATE SUMMER CHORES

In a country the size of the United States, flowering and the processes in the apiary can happen at very different times. Sometimes, several weeks can separate the various chores depending on where you live. But no matter where you live in the country, when there's no more nectar, it's time to prepare the colony for hibernation. This is also when you harvest the last honey, treat against Varroa mites, and provide the bees with winter feed. I usually perform all these steps within one to two weeks, depending on the weather.

THE FINAL HARVEST

Usually, I've already had time to harvest twice during summer. In mid-August, the nectar supply is finished in the area where I live. Then, I harvest one last time—sometimes a little earlier, sometimes later. If it's been a long, hot summer, I wait until the end of August. Again, it's the bees, the weather, and nature that influence my actions. No matter when you perform the last harvest, it should be done before it gets too cold outside, so you have time to provide the bees with winter feed. Beekeepers with several apiaries usually harvest earlier, so they have time to process all their honey.

For the final harvest, I lift out all the supers, and take the full frames hanging on the edges of the brood room. I leave an occasional frame with a little honey, so I don't have to give the bees winter feed immediately. If they've collected late, there's potentially some fall honey with hints of heather and honeydew in the hive. I don't want them to have any for winter; it contains substances that are difficult for bees to digest, increasing the risk of sickness during the winter months. It's better to fill their stores with the sugar solution that I give them. Sometimes, you can find honey that has crystallized in the cells. It's called cement honey and isn't suitable as a winter feed. This honey comes mainly from fir-needle pollen, is seasonal, and doesn't occur everywhere. You can cut pieces of honeycomb to eat as natural candy.

When I've harvested the honey, I can go through the colony in peace and quiet. Now I have to find the queen. If she is unlabeled, it can sometimes be difficult, especially if there are a lot of bees in the hive. But if there are eggs and larvae, it's a sign she should be in there somewhere. For winter, I want the colony to be really close together in a box. I retain one of the boxes that have acted as brood room and place the queen there. The idea is to remove the frames with dark wax in the brood room and replace them with nice frames with fresh, light wax. I select some of the finest wax frames from the extraction. If you don't have any extended frames, you can use frames with wax partitions. August tends to be a busy time for me: the kids go back to school, I have new projects at work, and more. If I have to wait to extract the honey for a few days or a week, I make sure to give the bees a little sugar solution so they don't starve. Meanwhile, I keep the supers in my shed, which is dry, warm, and closed to bees. It's good to store the honey in a warm place for a few days if the water content is too high and room temperature honey is also easier to extract.

Heather is one of summer's last draw plants, especially in the forest and in along the coast.

The bees should be living close to each other so they can keep warm during the winter. It's okay if they hang outside the hive in a cluster at first. When the temperature drops, they'll crawl inside.

Bees aren't happy when they lose their honey. If they get the opportunity, they'll gladly take back their hard-earned gold. A couple of years ago, while I was harvesting the last honey of the season, I noticed that the brilliant, sunny morning suddenly began to change. Large, dark, heavy rainclouds rolled in. It looked as if a thunderstorm was on its way. I hurried on with the harvesting, because you shouldn't be working with the hives when it's raining and thundering.

Just when I'd emptied the third and final hive and placed four honey supers under the protection of a bench for further transport, the sky opened. It had been a rainy summer, but this was probably the worst rain- and thunderstorm of the summer. I was forced to leave the supers under some provisional rain protection and quickly get indoors.

The next day, the sun shone again as if nothing had happened. I decided to deal with the work I'd begun the day before and do the extraction in the evening. Everything was quiet around my honey supers; only an occasional bee was buzzing around. When I carried the first honey super, I thought it felt unusually light. To my dismay, I noticed that almost all the frames were more or less empty of honey!

The storm had arrived so suddenly that I'd been in a hurry when I covered up the honey supers. The temporary storage solution and rain protection had some flaws, so my friends the bees had found a couple of small openings where they could get into the honey frames. Looters from three colonies had been flying back and forth all day and night between the hives and the supers to take back their honey. That summer, my honey harvest wasn't that great, but the bees were probably quite satisfied.

Cleaning and storing

After the final harvest, you need to clean all your equipment thoroughly and remove all the honey and wax residue from the tools. It will be nearly nine months before you'll need them again. Honey is antibacterial, but it's not fun to get unexpected visits because of the sweet remnants. Frames with dark wax (or wax that was broken into pieces during extraction) are collected and the wax melted. There are places that provide special wax melting services, where you can turn in your wax frames. Your frames will be melted, cleared, and cleaned. You get them back along with a package with new wax comb foundations, their weight equivalent to the weight of your submitted wax. On the Internet, you can also find drawings of simple solar wax melters and steam melters that you can build yourself. You can also cut out the wax itself, melt and clean it, and then send it away and have the embossed wax foundations sent back to you.

You then clean all the honey supers and empty, already melted frames. The supers have to be completely scraped clean of wax and propolis, then scorched with a propane torch or heat gun until the wood starts to change color. You can also wash them with a little dishwasher detergent and water, or 5% caustic soda solution. The frames also have to be scraped clean and boiled in the same solution. Bees don't like it when things are dirty around them, so there mustn't be any spots left. It's not enough if things are reasonably clean; they have to be spotless. Remember to dispose of the caustic soda solution responsibly; don't pour it out in nature. Intact extended wax frames that I'm using in the hives next season, I put inside cleaned honey supers which I stack on top of each other on a sheet of plywood in my cool storage space. Usually, I put newspaper between, over, and under each box—then I'm not risking that the wax is attacked by wax moths. Regular floor paper works well too. If you decide to store the boxes and frames in a storage space outside, you must protect them from mice.

If I've had a problem with decline in the number of bees and I suspect that the bees may have been infected by *Nosema*, I handle the extended frames in a different way. I stacks supers on top of each other, but without paper between. On top, I place an empty honey super and a bowl of acetic acid (not vinegar!). You can buy 60% to 80% acetic acid at the bee supply store. I put on something that can function as a lid, for example, a piece of plywood or a plastic tray that closes airtight. When the acetic acid comes into contact with the air, it evaporates, and the vapors from the acetic acid seep through the supers. This is an efficient way to kill both wax moths and Nosema spores that may remain in the honeycombs.

The big drone battle

The single task of a drone is to mate with the queen. After the mating act, which takes place in air, the drone falls dead to the ground. Life ends here for most drones; for others, it ends after the summer. The drones left in the colony are pushed out of the hive. Sometimes, you can even see a guard bee literally carry drones out of the hive. So, don't worry if there are a lot of dead bees outside the hive in late summer. It may seem cruel, but it's a necessity that will prevent the colony from perishing because of idle drones that devour the winter feed.

Formic acid against Varroa

After the final harvesting is the time to once again take action against Varroa. If you counted 5 to 10 dead mites per day when you checked the fallout in June, you have to treat your colonies with formic acid. The temperature should be below 77 °F (25 °C) when you do treatment. You can choose between short-term or long-term treatment. If you choose the latter, or if you wait a week or so with the short-term treatment, you have to give the bees a few pounds of support feed, so they don't starve (see page 90). It's also important to protect yourself well with rubber gloves and protective goggles when using formic acid.

For short-term treatment, open the hive and then place a washcloth on top of or under the frames. Distribute 60% formic acid on the washcloth with a dosing syringe, 0.006 ounces (2 ml) per frame. Leave the cloth in place for one or two days.

To perform a long-term treatment, you can use a formic acid evaporator and let the formic acid evaporate slowly over ten to twenty days. The concentration of formic acid that you should use depends on the evaporator. There's a simple way to effectively kill the mites: You buy the equipment from the bee supply store. Be sure to follow the instructions!

Hibernation—prepare for next season

After the final harvest, you may feel exhausted, but keep going! This is when you lay the foundation for next season, so you must ensure that the bees are properly cared for during the winter. The bees can hibernate in either one or two boxes—you have to adjust the size of the brood chamber to the size of the colony. If it's a strong and healthy colony (more than 20,000 bees), it can hibernate in two boxes; if it's an average or weak colony (20,000 or fewer members), it should hibernate in one box. Even the bee species is significant. In general, it's good for the colony to have a snug space for winter; the bees can stay warm easier and food is close at hand.

MERGING COLONIES

Remember that it's not about hibernating as many colonies as possible—it is the number of strong colonies that count. A strong colony is much more likely to survive a long cold winter than two weak ones. Don't be afraid to merge two weak colonies!

A strong and a weak colony: In the evening, place the box with the weaker colony on top of the stronger brood chamber, with a layer of newspaper in between. Don't forget to make some cuts with the hive tool in the paper so the bees have time to get used to each other's smell. When the bees have chewed their way through the paper, you'll have one single strong colony without any fuss. If there are two queens, you can opt to kill one; otherwise the bees will solve this themselves.

Two weak colonies: If you have two weak colonies or a couple of divided colonies, you can hibernate them on five frames each in the same box, and partition them with a wall. To do this, you'll need a partition wall and a bottom with two entrance openings. In this way, the colonies will help each other to stay warm inside the hive.

I'll take some of the wax frames in best condition from the extraction and use them for hibernation. If you don't have any extended frames, frames with wax partitions will work fine.

WINTER FEED—BOUGHT OR HOMEMADE

Sugar solution

Boil 1½ gallons (75.7 l) of water and 20 pounds (9.1 kg) of powdered sugar. Stir well so that all the sugar dissolves. Allow the sugar solution to cool so that it is lukewarm when you give it to the bees.

Quite soon after the end of the final extraction, you need to give the bees food to make up for the honey you have taken from them. Don't wait too long because the later you do, the greater the risk is that a cold spell will hit. If the temperature drops too low, the feed will solidify and it's too hard for the bees to pull it into the hive, or the bees will enter their winter cluster and then they don't accept feed. You can buy ready-mixed feed in the bee supply store. You'll need about 44 pounds (20 kg) per colony. You can also make your own 60% sugar solution by mixing two parts sugar and one part water. It takes about 35 pounds (16 kg) of powdered sugar to get 44 pounds (20 kg) of sugar solution. I alternate between both methods, depending on how much time I have. It's quite convenient to buy the finished feed and avoid having to stand and slop around in the kitchen. Whichever method you choose, you can supply the winter feed in several ways. But the process should not take more than three weeks, and it must be completed before the fall chill comes. Don't be stingy with winter feed! A colony that has plenty of food rarely starves to death during the winter. If there's leftover food in the spring, you can use it to create divisions.

If you have a smaller apiary, you can use a feed balloon with a feed cup placed on a feed board on top of the brood chamber. You have to refill it quite often because it only holds about a gallon (3.8 l) of sugar solution. I think it's a bit complicated and difficult to get clean. But its size makes it ideal for extra feed. The easiest and fastest way is to turn a food-grade storage bucket upside down or to fill a feed box.

Hibernation with feed bucket: Squeeze out the air using light pressure on the lid. Turn the bucket upside down and put it on top of the covering board's feed opening. In the middle of the bucket's lid are small holes where the sugar solution slowly seeps through so that the bees can lick it up and store it in the hive.

Don't wait too long to give the bees sugar solution after the final extraction. Instead of giving them the entire winter ration at once, you can split it up in portions.

Make sure the hive is level so the feed doesn't run out too quickly. Wipe off food that spills outside to avoid looting. Place an empty honey super on the hive so it forms a protective rim around the bucket. Add the lid. Check on the hives occasionally and make sure that the holes in the bucket aren't clogged. Remove the bucket after about three weeks or when it's empty.

Hibernation with bee feeder: You can buy a bee feeder from the bee supply store. Place it on the top box and pour in the sugar solution. Add the roof. You can leave the feeder in place over the winter to then easily be able to supply support feed in the same box in spring. Hibernation with a bee feeder can go fast; sometimes the bees can empty it in four to five days.

FALL AND WINTER TASKS

When you've extracted and poured the last of the year's honey harvest, placed your bees in hibernation, and given them enough winter feed, most of the year's bee activities are completed. All you have to do now is to ensure that the bees are warm and well in the hives and that the ventilation works as it should. The very last chore for the year is to treat against Varroa mites again.

Insulate and ventilate

The hives should be properly insulated so that the bees can keep warm in the winter—then they'll also need less feed. The ceiling and walls are most important. Most stacking hives that you buy have 1.2 inches (3 cm) of foam insulation in the walls and an insulated roof. If the hive isn't insulated, you have to take care of it in some way. My hive is not insulated; therefore I put in a couple of 2-inch- (5-cm-) thick foam boards along the short and long ends of the hive, and I also put one on as a lid.

A hive must also have good ventilation. When the bees burn energy, vapor forms that rises and can cause condensation. To catch the condensation, I cover the top boards of the hives sheets on all the hives with burlap. Some beekeepers use plastic or glass as top cover to be able to see how the bees develop without disturbing them. If you have such a cover, it's important that the hive is properly ventilated underneath so condensation doesn't form on the inner ceiling. I prefer to use cover boards of wood, where the air can pass between the cracks, or a cover board with a feeding opening and a net that can be covered if necessary. If the hives aren't well ventilated, the feed can turn moldy from moisture. Mold and moisture are among of the reasons why the bees can die in winter. My stacking hives have a mesh bottom that let in a lot of air.

In addition, each box has an adjustable bee emptier that I leave completely open. No matter what beekeepers around you say, allow the entrance to your hive to stay completely open during winter. If you have problems with birds, place chicken wire over the entrance. Also, remove the entrance board, which can gather a lot of snow that will clog the air supply. If you have problems with mice, you can put a queen excluder in front of the entrance. Some beekeepers sometimes put an empty box under the brood room with one or two empty frames for the bees to climb on. But it may be enough to make an extra high rim (2 to 2½ inches / 5–6.4 cm) between the bottom and the brood room.

Varroa treatment with oxalic acid

After feeding the bees, I can let them be for a while. To make sure my colonies are as free of Varroa mites as possible, I treat them with oxalic acid, which I prefer over other pesticides available for purchase. This treatment is the most effective of the ones you perform during the year, but you can only do it once and that is in the fall. You can basically do the treatment at any point during fall; the most important thing is that all the larvae have crawled out. I usually do it on a day when it's not windy, at the end of October or in the beginning of November. If you've placed your colony in hibernation in a box, the treatment is easy. At this time, the colony has started to form a winter cluster, which means that the treatment will go very smoothly. You open the hive and apply lukewarm oxalic acid solution with a syringe as evenly as possible on the bees crawling between the frames. The amount of oxalic acid you'll need varies depending on how big the colony is. A small colony needs 0.68 to 0.85 ounces (20–25 ml), a normal-sized requires 0.85 to 1 ounces (25–30 ml), and a large one 1.0 to 1.2 ounces (30–35 ml). If your colony is hibernating in two boxes, it gets a little more complicated: You'll have to open the hive and first drip the solution on the bees in the bottom box and then on the bees in the top box. Note that you should treat the bees with the same amount of oxalic acid per colony, whether it is hibernating in one box or two.

Oxalic acid solution

This batch is sufficient for about 10 colonies:

- 0.5 ounces (15 ml) of oxalic acid (found in paint stores)
- 0.8 cup (190 ml) lukewarm water
- 0.8 cup (190 ml) of sugar

Treatment with oxalic acid is a simple, cheap, and organic approach to combat Varroa mites. It feels a little melancholy when my daughters and I say goodbye to our bee friends for this season, but we'll see them again soon.

When the cold arrives

During winter, the inner core of the winter cluster maintains a temperature of 77 to 86 °F (25–30.6° C) and the outer edges are about 50 °F (10° C). So that all of the approximately 20,000 bees maintain an even temperature, they move slowly between the inner core and the outer edge. The bees thus don't sleep, and even this small amount of movement still requires energy, but the sugar solution acquired at hibernation is sufficient to be able to stay warm and have the energy for these small movements. Late winter is usually a difficult period for new beekeepers. I remember my first winter as quite challenging. I found it difficult to keep away from the hive. I wanted so much to make sure my little friends were doing well and had enough food. My care and zeal was probably the reason for the colony's destruction. The bees will do best if they're left alone. No matter how curious you are, refrain from disturbing the bees during the winter period—even in late winter. However, it might be good to visit your hives a couple of times to ensure that intrusive animals haven't overturned the hives. To make sure the roof doesn't blow away, you can put a big rock on it. Also, remove any branches that might be hanging down and hitting the hive, or anything else that may disturb the colony. If you live somewhere it snows a lot, make sure that the entrance is open so the bees can get air.

Also, be aware of what small hungry birds can be up to in late winter. They may have discovered that the hives hide a little food supply, and therefore they may be hanging out by the entrance. Great tit birds are probably the worst, knocking on the hive with their beaks and waiting until the sleepy, winter dazed bees come looking to see what is going on, only to suddenly become bird food. If you get a lot of problems with birds, you can build a cage of chicken wire to protect the entrance, or lean a board against the hive that covers the entrance and protects against early spring sun. If you have to move a hive a shorter distance in the garden, wait until the cleansing flight is completed in early spring. In summer it is primarily the hive's location that is important, not the hive itself, but during the winter months, the bees forget where the hive is standing.

Now, there's plenty of time to tend to things you didn't have time for earlier in the year. For example, you can mend broken frames or nail together new ones. You can also restring them and provide them with wax partitions—it's less than fun to thread frames when the hives are active full throttle. It's customary to calculate about forty frames per colony and you may need a couple of extra ones if the bees swarm or if you need to make a division. If you have access to a carpentry workshop, you can do major repairs now—or why not take the opportunity to build a new hive?

CHAPTER FIVE

HONEY, WAX, AND MORE

Honey is ideal for cooking and is a nutritious
sweetener. As if that wasn't enough, it also has
medicinal properties. You can choose between
different varieties and flavors in jars, or eat it as-is,
straight from the honeycomb. When you buy locally
produced honey, you support beekeeping while also
helping to promote biodiversity in your neighborhood.

REAL HONEY

Honey is a unique natural product that consists of fruit sugar (fructose), grape sugar (glucose), a little cane sugar (sucrose), and other sugars, water, and some percentage of enzymes, minerals and vitamins. For it to be called honey, nothing must be added or removed. What exactly may be marketed as honey is regulated by national laws. Carefully read the label when you buy honey in the store, especially when you buy liquid honey or honey with a particular flavor. Newly extracted honey is always liquid, translucent, and golden yellow to dark amber in color. It also contains many nutritious substances. Honey will eventually crystallize and become solid. This means that glucose crystals grow large. You see with the naked eye if the honey is highly crystallized. There is nothing wrong with it, but it can feel a little gritty in your mouth. High glucose levels speed up crystallization. If the glucose content is below 25 percent, like in acacia honey, it never crystallizes. In some stores, you can often find honey marked with the a beekeepers' association label. This marks a guaranteed quality product. The honey can come from small growers or from major honey producers who mix honey from several apiaries in order to offer a product of consistent quality, independent of whether the season has been good or bad, and that consumers recognize. Just as with wine and coffee, you can strive to benefit a wider range of honey in stores by buying local honey. This gives you the opportunity to experience the nuances of aroma and flavor that nature has to offer from that particular region. I always buy honey from small apiaries in different places I visit, at home and abroad—partly as a fun flavor memory, partly to support local beekeepers.

Newly extracted honey is liquid but becomes solid over time. Acacia honey never solidifies. You can get solid honey to stay liquid for a shorter or longer time, depending on the type, by heating it rapidly to about 104 °F (40° C) in a water bath. If you heat the honey to temperatures higher than this, some of its nutritional value will decrease.

Color, flavor, and different kinds of honey

I keep my hives in a classical residential area that has lots of flowerbeds, berry bushes, and old fruit trees. Honey obtained from flowers is called flower honey or floral honey. Its flavor is often a mixture of the different plants of the season and it's most often light yellow in color. Anyone who has hives in or near densely forested areas can get forest honey (also called leaf honey). Forest honey has the color of dark syrup and a fairly strong flavor with hints of caramel. The color and flavor of the honey also depends on when in the season you're harvesting it. Honey from the peak of summer is light and has a floral flavor. The harvest is usually smaller because the bees use most of it themselves to build up the colony in the spring. High summer honeys normally give the biggest harvest of the season. The color can be light yellow to amber depending on which flowers are dominant. Often, the honey has a wide register of flavors: clover, raspberry, blueberry, and wildflowers.

In some areas, heather honey is often harvested; it's also called fall honey. It may have some hints of leaf honey (if late summer has been warm) and is dark amber, with a rather sharp taste.

NATURAL FLAVORS IN HONEY

If you harvest frequently and according to plant flowering times, you can get naturally flavored honey with its taste and scent from a particular flower and has nothing to do with artificial flavoring. Dandelion honey, rapeseed honey, clover honey, heather honey, linden honey, and raspberry honey are good examples. Artificially flavored honey exists, but it needs to be clearly labeled as such. One year, my honey had clear hints of mint in it. But the small mint plant in my flowerbed could hardly have given flavor to the whole honey harvest. After some research, I realized that my bees had probably found their way to an old castle with a large Linden tree avenue. Linden honey is flavorful with a fresh touch of mint.

The color and taste of the honey depends on which flowers the bees have collected nectar from. It also impacts how long the honey stays liquid.

Honey tasting

Invite your friends to a honey tasting lunch in the countryside. It'll be a fun way to explore the complex flavors of honey, from buttery caramel tones and fresh mint to flowering clover meadow. Use your own honey if you can and also buy as many different varieties you can find from beekeepers near and far.

When the bees collect nectar from flowers, tiny pollen particles are also always included and end up in the honey. With the use of a microscope, the pollen particles make it possible to determine from what plants the honey has been derived. To be called raspberry honey, for example, you must be able to trace at least 50 percent of the pollen from raspberry flowers. On the other hand, you can write "early summer honey with dandelion" on your honey labels with a pollen content of only 30 percent.

If you want to immerse yourself in pollen analysis or simply just want to know where your bees collected the nectar for your honey, there are courses you can enroll in. Your local beekeepers' association will help you.

Storage

Honey has a very long shelf life. If you're going to sell your honey, the industry recommends that you set an expiration date two years after the date you extracted it. Archaeologists, who in the early 1900s explored the Egyptian Pharaohs' tombs, actually found honey inside the tombs that was still perfectly edible. The high sugar content (80 percent) in the honey acts as a preservative. Honey should be stored in a dark place and at a uniformly low temperature, preferably below 59 °F (15 °C). If you intend to store it for a long time, it's also fine to keep it inside the refrigerator. If you freeze newly extracted honey, it will stay liquid for a while after you thaw it out again. The honey that you use daily can be stored at room temperature—that's when its taste and aroma is at its best. The use of honey in tea is healthy, but you should wait to add it until the tea has cooled, since the effects of its various nutritional substances will diminish in temperatures above 104 °F (40 °C). Many of them also disappear when the honey is aging, so be sure to consume newly extracted honey when it's fresh—that's when it tastes the best.

The honey to the left in the picture has been stored in a place that was too cool, so that glucose crystals have formed on the inside of the glass jar. The jar to the right has been stored in a place that was too warm, which has caused the honey to separate.

Honey stored in excessive heat slowly begins to separate or stratify. This means that most of the grape sugar sinks to the bottom, while a smaller amount of fruit sugar settles on top as a clear golden liquid. There's nothing wrong with honey that's separated. Just stir the jar to get a smooth texture, then it'll be as new again. The separation increases the water content slightly in the surface layer of the honey, which may mean that over time, the honey will begin to ferment. Fermented honey smells a bit like beer, but it's not dangerous to eat and will do just fine for baking and cooking. In order to stop the fermentation, put honey in the refrigerator. If the honey has a water content higher than 20 percent, it can also begin to ferment. If the water content is less than 20 percent or if the honey has been stored in temperatures that are too low, the crystallization process may cause it to develop a frost-looking pattern on the inside of the glass. There's absolutely nothing wrong with the honey—you can continue using it as usual. The "frost" is glucose crystals and changes neither the flavor nor the quality of the honey.

Healing and nourishing properties

Honey is naturally antibacterial and antifungal. A week after extracting, it contains lactic acid bacteria and a small amount of hydrogen peroxide, a strong disinfectant substance that helps wound heal. That's why honey isn't used just as a sweetener and in cooking, but also in various health cures and as medical treatment. It's also an ingredient of various body care products such as shampoos, skin creams, and more. One of my neighbors uses my honey, not only because she thinks it tastes good, but also because she washes her hair with it. She felt that her hair got too dry from ordinary hair products, but after doing a hair mask with honey, it became soft and smooth again. If you try this yourself, use a locally produced or organic honey that hasn't been heated; the honey will retain its healing properties.

Use the wax

When you have your own apiary, you don't generate only honey, you can also take advantage of the wax and use it in various homemade products. I usually gather all the residual wax after the uncapping and straining and then I melt it in boiling water in an old, big pot. The lighter wax settles on the surface while any debris will sink to the bottom. If there's a lot of debris in the wax, I swaddle it in a piece of clean cotton fabric and put it at the bottom of the pan with a weight on top. I then fill the pot up with water and boil it. In this way, the wax is filtered in through the fabric. From the melted wax I make several things, including ointment or lip balm, candles, and furniture polish. You can make the beeswax ointment from the basic recipe in the margin, but there are many variations. If you want to make lip balm, mix in more wax so that consistency is harder, and add a little bit of vitamin E. Experiment and try using other oils than rapeseed, but avoid mixing in essential oils.

Beeswax is a fantastic natural product that can be used for lots of things, for example ointments. Sometimes, we make beeswax candles for Christmas. When we want to splurge, we make fancier candles by rolling honeycombs around a wick, a popular craft with my daughters. Beeswax candles emit much less soot than regular candles.

Beneficial bacteria

Researchers in Lund have identified several new, living lactic acid bacteria in bees' honey stomachs. This supposedly protects the bees against various diseases and is also found in honey. This bacterium has successfully healed horses suffering from antibiotic-resistant Staph infections. The active substances produced by lactic acid bacteria are present in fresh honey. When it comes to honey, newly extracted honey—especially heather honey—appears to have the most active substances.

Beeswax ointment

2.7 ounces (75 g) beeswax

0.8 cups (190 ml) canola oil

1 teaspoon (5 ml) honey

0.68 ounces (20 ml) propolis extract

For the ointment, I heat wax and canola oil in a beaker or in a large glass in a pot of water on the stove. When everything has melted, I take the beaker from the water bath and allow the mixture to cool until it starts to get a little cloudy. I stir constantly with a spoon to avoid clumps. I then add honey and propolis extract and mix well. Finally, I pour the cream into jars and let it cool slowly, sitting in lukewarm water.

You can also make other products from beeswax. My mom likes to renovate old furniture as a hobby. To bring up the shine in wooden furniture, she rubs them with a furniture polish made from beeswax, linseed oil, and gum turpentine. Prior to using the polish, she dusts off and wipes down the surfaces. She then works in small amounts of the creamy polish with a soft, clean cloth in the longitudinal direction of the wood until most of it has penetrated the surface. Too much polish can cause sticky spots that are hard to remove. The rags you've used should be incinerated or placed in an airtight bag before being thrown away because linseed oil is highly flammable.

Furniture polish

1 part beeswax

1 part boiled linseed oil

1 part gum turpentine

SVEA'S HONEY COOKIES

My daughter loves to bake and experiment with different ingredients.
Sometimes she outdoes herself. Few cookies are as irresistible
as these. Svea's honey cookies are criminally good.

1. Preheat the oven to 350 °F (175 °C).

2. Stir together butter, sugar, honey, and vanilla into in a bowl.
   Mix flour and baking powder in a separate bowl, mix into
   the batter, and stir to form a dough.

3. Shape two long strips of dough and place them on
   parchment paper on a baking sheet. Flatten the strips
   with your hand.

4. Put the baking sheet in the oven and bake the cookies for
   15 minutes. Take them out and cut them into angled, oblong
   cookies. Let cool.

*This recipe makes
about 30 cookies*

½ cup (120 ml) butter

½ cup (120 ml) granulated sugar

3½ tablespoons (52 ml)
   liquid honey

1 teaspoon (5 ml) vanilla extract

¾ cup (180 ml) all-purpose flour

½ teaspoon (2.5 ml) baking
   powder

SARA'S GRANOLA

During the winter, we usually have oatmeal with a bit of honey in the mornings. In the summer, when there are more fresh berries, we prefer yogurt with berries and homemade granola. And naturally, we put newly harvested liquid honey on top.

Makes about 17 cups (4 l) granola

2 Tablespoons (30 ml) sunflower oil

½ cup (120 ml) maple syrup

4 Tablespoons (60 ml) liquid honey

1 teaspoons (5 ml) vanilla extract

2½ cups (600 ml) rolled oats

¾ cup (180 ml) hazelnuts

½ cup (120 ml) sunflower seeds, shelled

½ cup (120 ml) pumpkin seeds, shelled

¾ cup (180 ml) raisins or dried goji berries

1. Preheat the oven to 350°F (175° C).

2. Mix together oil, maple syrup, honey, and vanilla in a large bowl. Add the oats and mix well.

3. Spread the mixture evenly on the baking sheet in one or two roasting pans and toast it in the oven for 20 minutes or until the oats have a golden yellow color. Let cool.

4. Chop the hazelnuts coarsely and roast them in a hot, dry frying pan. Mix all the nuts with the rest of the ingredients in a large bowl. Pour into a pretty glass jar with a tight lid.

GÖTA'S HONEY PUFFS

We had a large bag of puffed rice that no one seemed to be able to finish. Instead of making muffins, Göta wanted to make honey puffs. She created these cookies, filled with healthy seeds.

1. Preheat the oven to 350 °F (175 °C).

2. Toast the sunflower seeds in a hot, dry pan. Do the same with the pumpkin and sesame seeds, but make sure they don't burn. Mix the seeds with the puffed rice in a large bowl. Melt the butter in a small saucepan over low heat. Take the pan from the heat and add honey. Stir until the honey has dissolved. Pour the honey butter over the seeds and puffed rice, and mix to a smooth batter.

3. Put the batter into paper baking cups in a muffin tin or on parchment paper on a baking sheet. Bake the honey puffs in the oven for 7 or 8 minutes, or until lightly browned. Store in a jar with a tight lid.

Makes about 30 cookies

½ cup (120 ml) sunflower seeds, shelled

½ cup (120 ml) pumpkin seeds, shelled

4 tablespoons (60 ml) sesame seeds

2 cups (475 ml) toasted puffed rice

¼ cup (60 ml) butter

½ cup (120 ml) firm honey

HONEY MUSTARD

Easy to make and to vary, this mustard works well as-is with Christmas ham, or you can flavor it with thyme, tarragon, chili, horseradish, whiskey, or whatever you like. Make the mustard well in advance of the holidays and store it in the refrigerator.

Makes about 2 cups (475 ml) mustard

3½ Tablespoons (50 ml) yellow mustard seed

1½ Tablespoons (22 ml) brown mustard seeds

4 Tablespoons (60 ml) honey

1 Tablespoons (15 ml) vinegar (12 % solution)

½ cup (120 ml) water

1 teaspoons (5 ml) salt

COARSE HONEY MUSTARD

1. Mix the mustard seeds with a hand blender or crush them in a mortar. Add honey and vinegar and continue to mix while adding water, one drop at a time. The mustard should be creamy but still have some whole grains remaining. Season with salt.

2. Let the mustard rest in the fridge for at least 12 hours. If it gets too thick, you can dilute it with water. Pour into clean jars and store in the refrigerator.

Makes about ½ cup (120 ml) mustard

2 Tablespoons (30 ml) Colman's mustard powder

2 Tablespoons (30ml) liquid honey

2 teaspoons (10 ml) apple cider vinegar

Shredded peel and juice from ½ lime, orange, or lemon (optional)

SPICY HONEY MUSTARD

1. Mix mustard powder, honey and vinegar. If you want, you can season it with zest and juice from lime, orange, or lemon.

2. Pour the mustard into jar, put on a lid, and let stand in refrigerator for an hour before serving.

JOACHIM'S SPICY HONEY BREAD

In the autumn, after the final honey harvest and hibernation of my colonies, I usually use more honey in baking. This is a bread with a spicy taste to match strong and tasty dishes—and for the evening tea.

1. Dissolve the yeast in the water in a small bowl and let stand for about five minutes.

2. Mix honey, coriander, cinnamon and cloves in a bowl. Add the yeast mixture and stir together. Add the milk. Add flour, a little at a time, and finally mix in the salt. Knead for 5 to 10 minutes to form a smooth dough. Cover with plastic wrap or a kitchen towel and let rise in a warm place for 30 minutes.

3. Lightly flour a large clean kitchen towel, put the dough on it and shape it into a square. Fold in the sides of the dough toward the center and then fold it across so that it becomes a square package. Wrap the dough in the towel and let rise for 30 minutes.

4. Preheat the oven to 485 °F (250 °C) and place a glass or metal tray with some ice cubes in the bottom of the oven. Stretch the dough and fold it again, in the same way you did earlier. Divide the dough in two, shape into two elongated breads and place on a baking sheet with parchment paper. Cover with a kitchen towel and let rise in a warm, draft-free place for 1 hour. Bake the bread for about 45 minutes. Open the door after 15 minutes and release the steam. Reduce the heat to 395 °F (200 °C). Remove the loaves and let them cool on a rack in a towel.

Makes two oblong loaves

1½ tablespoons (22 ml) dry yeast

1½ cups (360 ml) lukewarm water

½ cup (120 ml) honey

1 teaspoon (5 ml) ground coriander

½ teaspoon (2.5 ml) ground cinnamon

½ teaspoon (2.5 ml) ground cloves

3 teaspoons (15 ml) salt, preferably sea salt

¾ cup (180 ml) milk at room temperature

5½ cups (720 ml) all-purpose flour

BARBECUED RIBS WITH HONEY GLAZE

I learned to make ribs this way from a neighbor who is
a real barbecue pro. The secret to getting juicy ribs is to
boil thick ribs in broth a day in advance.

Makes 4 servings

2½ pounds (1.1 kg) ribs

2 bay leaves

1 teaspoon (5 ml) ground black pepper

1 tablespoon (15 ml) allspice

1 onion

1 carrot

2 cloves garlic

4½ cups (1 l) water

2 teaspoons (10 ml) salt

Spicy honey glaze

3 tablespoons (45 ml) honey

2 tablespoons (30 ml) olive oil

2 tablespoons (30 ml) oyster sauce

2 garlic cloves, chopped

1 tablespoon (15 ml) Chinese soy sauce

1 tablespoon (15 ml) sambal oelek

1 tablespoon (15 ml) tomato paste

Juice of 1 lime

Dried chili to taste

DAY 1

1. Crush bay leaves, black pepper, and allspice in a mortar.

2. Peel and cut the onion, carrot, and garlic cloves in large pieces.

3. Put the pieces and ribs in a big saucepan. Cover with water and add the spice mixture. Bring to a boil, skim, and add salt. Simmer for 50 minutes.

4. Let the ribs remain in the broth and keep cool overnight.

DAY 2

1. Light the grill.

2. Mix all the ingredients for the honey glaze.

3. Remove the ribs from the pan, wipe them lightly, and brush them on all sides with glaze.

4. Put the ribs on the grill and barbecue them for about 10 minutes on each side or until they seem done. The cooking time varies depending on the thickness of the ribs. Serve with roasted potato wedges and coleslaw.

THANK YOU

In autumn of 2013 the seeds were sown for a book about bees and beekeeping, not just for aspiring beekeepers, but for everyone who is curious about bees. One evening in May, after the annual spring party at Bonnier Nonfiction Publishing, I decided to make the book happen. It wouldn't have been possible without Bonnier Nonfiction and, above all, my inquisitive, zealous, and patient editor, Susanna Eriksson Lundqvist, and my deeply engaged publisher Martin Ransgart, who believed in the idea, and that I would be able to implement it in such a short time. A big reason for why the book turned out so beautifully is my friend and the book's photographer, Roland Persson, who literally crawled into the hive to get the perfect shot—of these, there were many. I would also like to thank my knowledgeable facts reviewers, Preben Kristiansen and Lotta Fabricius Kristiansen, who know about most things related to beekeeping, bee health, and honey processing. Thank you also for allowing me to toss my words around with the copywriter star, Hans Malm. And thank you, Emilie Crispin Ekstrom, for allowing me to vent questions about fonts and design. I also want to thank Victoria who is and old friend from junior high school, for translating my book. My interest in bees was awakened by my mother's cousin, Eskil Ringström, and his father. My first hive would never have been built if not for my grade school woodworking teacher, Elmer, who let me build it from a drawing by Lars-Olov Kullberg. As a beginner, I asked many silly bee questions—we all need to be allowed to do so. Luckily, there are accommodating beekeepers such as Kjell Andersson and Bengt Haglund. If you live in a residential area, you're also happy to have sympathetic neighbors who don't get afraid when the bees swarms. Thanks to the Ihrborg family; and to Sara Moberg, for teaching me that you can wash your hair, face, and body with honey. My family's support throughout the writing process has been crucial: my mother, Ulla Petterson, always believed in me and was also been a zealous text reviewer. My sister Joanna Petterson was a proud supporter; my eldest sister, Jessica Kewenter Kullberg, gave the gift of close contact with the bees as a child and let me use her house in Skåne to write this book. Thank you to mother-in-law Eva Andersson for lending me the straw hive, and taking time to test the recipes. My beloved daughters: the perfectionist Svea and the expressionist Göta skillfully reproduced the movement of a swarm of bees in one single image and helped me to draw headline font Svea Sans. In closing, I want to thank my wife, Sara, for her drawings and lovely dry pastels of bees and flowers that gave the book extra warmth. She is a special person who's close to me and has always supported me. Last but not least—a big thank you to all our bees.

INDEX

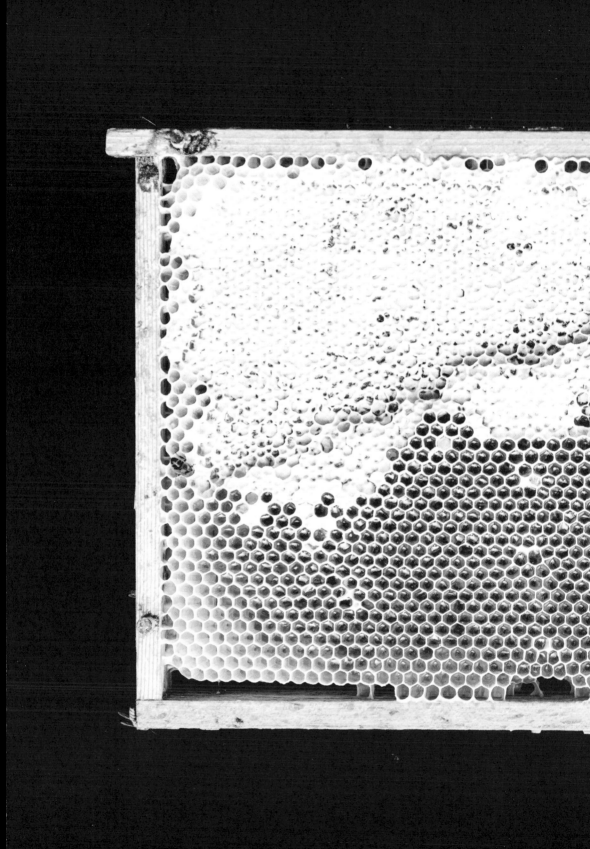